Rescue Me, Sweet Jesus

*Letters and Prayers to the God of Comfort
for All Those Who Are Suffering*

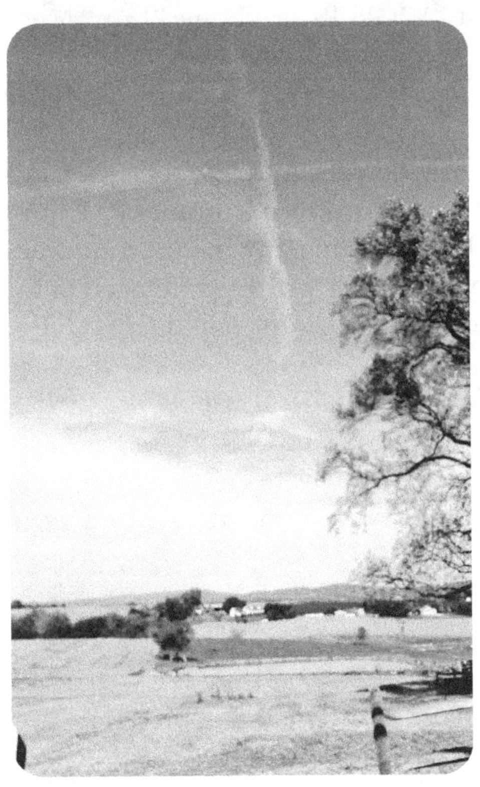

Patricia Anne "Patti" Meitzler Davis

ISBN 979-8-88644-304-2 (Paperback)
ISBN 979-8-88644-305-9 (Digital)

Covenant Books
11661 Hwy 707
Murrells Inlet, SC 29576
www.covenantbooks.com

Rescue Me, Sweet Jesus

A Prayer of Suffering, Endurance, Faith, and Hope

O Lord, my soul cries out to you from the depths of my pain and anguish.

I am but a prisoner in my own body, wanting to be released from my unrelenting pain and sin of this world.

I am but a small raft in a vast ocean, trying to stay afloat but slowly sinking with the ocean swallowing me up.

Rescue me, sweet Jesus, from the torment and pain that I'm in, for only you can save me; no one else can.

I long for you, Jesus, for your healing touch and unconditional love to pull me up and restore my life unto me.

I live in fear of the future, of what my life will be, hanging on day by day through so many tears; will I have to endure days, months, or even years?

I am so weak, I do not feel strong; in this world, I truly don't belong.

You are my hope and my only source of strength.

I cry and cry through my physical pain; thank You, Jesus, for being the lamb that was slain.

It is my eyes, the windows to my soul, that grow dim waiting for You to free me; I only ask, when?

I see God's beauty, which surrounds me, yet I cannot feel—longing for Jesus to take away my brokenness and rescue me still.

My torn and tattered body—so weary to go on, yet I know that it is to You, my Lord and Savior Jesus, that I truly belong.

You took the cross and suffered such pain, died for our sins, and took all of our blame.

Rescue me, sweet Jesus, from the torment and pain that I'm in, for only You can wash me clean of sin.

A prisoner to my pain, not wanting to go on, I remember You, Lord Jesus, and how You suffered so long.

I long for heaven, my eternal home, where You will comfort and wrap Your loving arms around me.

There, I will behold the beauty that my eyes will see.

You will wipe away all of my tears, and the pain of this life will be gone.

I will sing and worship You, Lord, with praises and majestic song.

I long to meet You, Jesus, and walk through that door into eternal glory and be freed from this imperfect world.

Sin has damaged my body and ravages me with so much pain that I am unable to escape; only thoughts of heaven can fill my soul with peace and with Your unending grace.

How I long to be with You, Jesus, in that most beautiful place.

Only You, sweet Jesus, can rescue me—no one else can; I can't see my purpose in Your wonderful master plan.

Please, Lord, have mercy on me and take this pain from me, if it be your will, for all I do now is cry and try to hold on to each day still.

Please, Jesus, take my hand, as only You can, for I fear I am drowning in the world's terrible quicksand.

It is only You, Lord, who can restore me, who my mind and body long to see.

I pray for strength, courage, and endurance that only comes from You, Lord, above; I long to feel Your healing touch and Your forever undying love.

Please, Lord, send Your heavenly angels of light to come and carry me into Your loving arms; it is only there that I can truly rest, free of evil and all harm.

Rescue me, sweet Jesus, from the torment and pain that I'm in, for only Your love and grace will continually sustain me time and time again; I need Your healing hand upon me to enjoy my life again.

> *You are my hiding place, You will protect me from*
> *trouble and surround me with songs of deliverance.*
> —Psalm 32:7–8

> *When the righteous cry for help, the Lord hears,*
> *and rescues them from all their troubles.*
> —Psalm 34:17

> *And in the fourth watch of the night, Jesus*
> *went unto them, walking on the sea.*
> *But straightway Jesus spoke unto them, saying,*
> *Be of good cheer, it is I, be not afraid.*
> —Matthew 14:25, 27

Jesus, Mighty Lord and King

A Prayer of Praise and Thanksgiving

The Lord is my helper; He shall not forsake me.

He sends guardian angels in my friends that surround me.

When I am scared, He is my comforter, giving me blessed reassurance with His love and with His peace.

When I am in pain and suffering, He will not be far but very near, carrying me through the darkness while quieting my fears.

For the Lord is good and kind and says, "Seek and you shall find."

He knocks on the door of my heart, waiting patiently to be invited in because His love is so perfect and has no end.

Against the enemy, I will stand and will never lose, as my Lord gives me His strong, powerful, helping hand.

The enemy must flee at the name of Jesus, my king; hearts will rejoice, and songs I will sing to Jesus, who covers me under His mighty wing.

Evil must be gone, as the Lamb, He will come—bringing salvation and hope.

His light will be bright, so I can stand and fight the darkness of this world.

I will not stumble and fall, for my Lord is there, and on His name, I will call.

He will save me and bring me to glory, where there is no sickness, pain, or tears.

He will crush all my enemies and all of my fears and will not let any harm come to me.

And one day, I will be with Him, and my eyes, they will see heaven—that beautiful place that the Lord has prepared for me.

Together, we are all journeying through this life and, with God's help, will choose the path that is right.

Our roads are all different but equally as hard, but do not fear, for our Lord and God, He is with us and will always draw near.

He knows life is tough and says, "My grace is enough."

He always gives us help along life's difficult path.

God's angels, they are among us, and one day, we will ride on their wings to our one true heavenly home.

There, Jesus will smile and reign, welcoming us, as He sits with His crown of glory on His most majestic throne.

The Lord your God in your midst, the Mighty One, will save;
He will rejoice over you with gladness, He will quiet you
with his love, He will rejoice over you with singing.
—Zephaniah 3:17

In the Arms of Jesus

A Prayer of Suffering and Faith

From the depths of my soul, I cry out to You, Jesus; please end my suffering and set me free.

It is You, Lord, the only one who can read my heart and truly see just how hard the pain of this life has been for me.

Please, Jesus, draw near to my side,
for You're the only one who knows how many tears I've cried.

The life that I once knew is no more, for my flesh is tormented with sickness and pain,

and I can no longer do the things I once loved; nothing is the same.

Even as my life belongs to You and not to me, I want to fly free on the wings of a dove—

to fly to You on a soft white cloud that carries me to heaven, where I will be healed in total body of all sickness and of pain, where you will wipe away my tears and I will never ever have another fear.

In the arms of Jesus is where I want to be,
to look into Your comforting eyes and see the love divine of Thee.

   PATRICIA ANNE "PATTI" MEITZLER DAVIS

Even in my painful body, I will give You thanksgiving and praise, for I know life is a gift that can be taken away so untimely and so quick.

You've given me so many blessings throughout my life that, sometimes, I forget when the road becomes so dark and painful; all I can feel is life's strife.

Please, Jesus, draw near to my side,
for You're the only one who knows how many tears I've cried.

Jesus, I will give You blessing and honor, even when I feel that I can't hold on any longer.

I pray, when I am too weak to go on, You will hold on to me and carry me across life's most difficult roads.

You will give me a sense of peace that it is my Lord and Savior who holds me up, for this I will surely know.

In the arms of Jesus is where I want to be,
to look into Your comforting eyes and see the love divine of Thee.

Your unconditional love is a free gift from You to me. Please help me on my darkest days to open my eyes so I will really see and have no doubts but truly believe.

Your kind and gentle, loving words penetrate my soul and make me want to continue with You on this painful journey of life with you by my side, holding my hand,

knowing I can't get up, except only by Your strength; eventually, I will stand.

Please, Jesus, draw near to my side,
for You're the only one who knows how many tears I've cried.

I feel trapped in my broken body with no way out; thank You, Lord, for asking me to trust and not to doubt.

In the arms of Jesus is where I want to be,
to look into Your comforting eyes and see the love divine of Thee.

Please, Jesus, don't ever let me go, for I never want to be separated from Your unconditional kindness and consistently unfailing grace and love.
The tears I shed through so much pain, knowing my earthly life will never be the same.
I have to trust that God has a plan, even though I can't see it or begin to understand.

Please, Jesus, draw near to my side,
for You're the only one who knows how many tears I've cried.

So many nights, I sit up crying, praying, and just asking why.
Then I realize through all my pain, Jesus comforts the ones who suffer alongside of Him.
My suffering has brought me closer in relationship with Him,
for it is on His name that He wants me to lean and depend on.
O Lord, my deepest prayers are sent to You in heaven on a kiss of the wind,
for I believe in Your healing, Jesus; I know that you can.
If I never get healed in this life, I know one day I will be with You in perfect paradise.
I'll feel your healing love, and my soul will be escorted to heaven by angels on the wings of a beautiful white dove.

For it is in the arms of Jesus that I truly want to be;
I look into Your ever so comforting eyes, and behold, the glory, I see
and know that I will be forever healed and spend glorious eternity with Thee.

*I have spoken these things to you so that you shall have peace in Me.
You shall have suffering in the world, but take
heart, I have overcome the world.*

—John 16:33

My Beautiful Journey Home

An Inspiration of Hope, Peace, and Comfort

How I long to be in the presence of my true Lord—Jesus.

I want to feel His comforting embrace around my painfully broken body that I've not been able to escape from.

I have longed to stand before Him, feeling His warm, radiant beauty and everlasting love in a most beautiful place.

A love so pure and true, it's snow-white, like that of the softest winged dove;

I take a breath and gently close my eyes, waiting for Jesus to carry me to heaven above.

In a blink of an eye, I'm looking at the most wondrous, peaceful sea that God has ever meant for my eyes to see.

The water is so blue and ever so calm that, in this moment, I realize my soul truly belongs.

Colorful tiny fragments of sea glass glisten on the sand, like small fine diamonds basking in the warm rays of the sun.

Seeing the beauty around me that God has created, I marvel at its majestic presence, even in all my pain and brokenness.

The clear blue sky is filled with soft, fluffy clouds, and the sand is ever so white;

I can hardly behold the beauty that God has allowed to fill my sight.

As the crystal cool water ebbs and flows in perfect rhythm, I see the snowy whitecaps softly lapping at my feet.

Feeling such joy, my heart is overwhelmed with great peace.

Breathing in the warm salt air, I realize I'm all alone gazing at this breathtaking blue sea; as I look up, my Lord and Savior Jesus is walking toward me.

He's smiling with such a deep love on His face that I fall on my knees worshipping Him at His once nail-driven feet.

He gently helps me up, takes my hand, and softly says:

Come, my precious child, and walk with Me.

His luminous smile and comforting eyes emanate amazing love and such peaceful grace that all I want to do is gaze upon my Lord's holy face.

My diseased, painful body makes it hard for me to walk and to breath.

It is then that Jesus lovingly picks me up and begins to carry me.

He carries me along the majestic shoreline that seems to never end.

Safe in His arms, I feel the warm breezes brush across my face from the quiet summer wind.

I begin to see images of my life flash before my eyes, painted in serene colors across the tropical sky.

Some scenes are happy, some are sad, some are dark and, other times, are bright;

Jesus tells me that every season of my life, He was always there with me through every day and every dark night.

I express that I feel so safe and comforted in His arms—feelings of complete love and safety from all harm.

I speak to Jesus of how I've longed all of my life to see Him.

My recurring earthly thoughts and images of how this would be just Jesus and me, spending time along God's seashore of tranquility.

As He gazes down at my tired and painful face, He continues to carry me across the sands of the sea ever so lovingly.

I talk about my life and thank Him for forgiving all of my sins.

I tell Him how my one true desire is to be in relationship and always to be with Him.

As we, together, watch the sun start to fade and see the sun setting over the water, I acknowledge Him as my faithful and eternal Father.

He smiles and says to me:

> *I am the alpha and the omega, the beginning and the end.*
>
> *My precious little child, throughout your life, I've always heard your prayers.*
>
> *It was I who was there when you felt no one else cared.*
>
> *When everything in your world was falling apart, it was I who sent kisses of whispers, reminding just how much I have always loved you.*
>
> *I have always been here and never left your side, for it was in Me that I taught you to trust and always to abide.*
>
> *Suffering with much pain, I saw how the storms of life became so rough that you couldn't bear to go on; My unconditional love was sustaining when you were so weak and just couldn't be strong.*
>
> *A sea of tears I know you have cried, and there were many days that I know you just wanted to die, not able to bear the burden of your suffering anymore.*
>
> *Forever so long, your faith continued, hearing My comforting voice in words and in beautiful song, thus giving strength, sustaining you all along.*

*When your pain and agony of the world
became just too much, I reached down and softly
pulled you to Me and closed your weary eyes, for I
saw your anguish, and I heard your cries.*
*I brought you to this beautiful place because
I've always known your love for the sea;*
*It was here that I knew you had so many times
found Me.*

As moonbeams now twinkled on the glistening tides, I glance up and see small bright stars in the midnight sky, their reflection dancing on the water, as if points of light were reaching down from heaven above.

Hearing the soft waves and rhythm of the sea, I continue to bask in the arms and safety of my Savior's unfailing love.

Growing more weary with pain, I look down to see my Lord's hands—where they were once pierced and bloodstained.

I thanked and praised Him for all He had done and given to me.

Then I explained how truly sorry I was, for on many days, the agony of constant debilitating pain had weakened my faith, causing me to doubt, when I should have believed.

Jesus smiled and told me how He unconditionally loved and had always forgiven me.

He asked if I was ready to go home to heaven to dwell with Him eternally, where all things would be made new—

No more sickness, pain, anxiety, or disease ever again.

There, I believed I would be healed completely, as He said:

I have already prepared a place for you.

Yes—it was my true heart's desire that when my life had come to an end, I wanted to go and live with Him, not only as my one true Father but also as Jesus, my friend.

As I thanked Him for my amazing journey home, I closed my eyes once again, and Jesus carried me across the moonlit sea and into heaven's eternity.

Still in His arms, awakened from sleep, I beheld the splendor of perfect heavenly beauty and such eternal peace.

My Savior looked lovingly down on me, smiled and whispered:

My precious little one, you are now home.
Shalom [peace].

He will wipe away every tear from their eyes.
There will be no more death or mourning or crying or
pain, for the old order of things has passed away.
—Revelation 21:4

My Angel in Disguise

An Inspiration of Suffering, Friendship, and Gratitude

To my best friend, Lisa

I have a wonderful friend, who has always been by my side in life's most severe trials—personal illness and debilitating pain.

She knows; she suffers terribly and, most days, is confined to her bed.

Similar backgrounds we both do have, once living our days with so much joy;

now, illness and pain have made us so sad.

An example of Christlike kindness is she, extending her loving hand and her heart to a friend or family member in need.

Never is she judgmental but always patient and kind.

Truly, she's a gem and, to me, a rare find.

God sends us angels in disguise—to help us through our sorrows, pain, and unbearable suffering.

I love my friend because she's an encourager, gentle, and always so kind.

Journeying down life's difficult road, our loving God sends special people to help us in our time of need.

God plants a small seed and nurtures it with His love and His great sovereignty.

He watches how it grows and blooms into a beautiful friendship between two friends that become so true and wise.

In her, God sends me an angel in disguise.

She's always there to lift me up when I shed painful tears and have so many fears.

Shared suffering and sickness bring people together, especially if one person can truly relate to what another person is feeling, both physically and emotionally.

We look to God for healing, and when it's delayed or it doesn't seem to come, we ask each other why, for neither of us can see God's purpose or understand His lifelong plan.

When we feel we cannot or do not want to endure another day, we're here lifting each other up with encouraging words and phrases such as:

"You can do this!

Live another day and fight!

You know you can and are coping with this, whether you see it or not!

God doesn't want you to give up."

A constant battle just to live each day; with God's help, we both really try.

Sickness and pain know no age, gender, or boundaries.

We cry out to our Lord:

"Please, please, remove our thorns from our sides that's causing so much anguish and heart-wrenching agony—

Like a tornado roaring through, destroying everything in sight, not just our bodies but also our will to fight.

It also devastates social and family relationships of people that once cared for us but just don't understand our sickness."

In depression, we isolate ourselves, not wanting our loved ones to see our true sadness, all the discomfort and pain we cannot hide from our faces.

Leaving in its wake are depressed, broken, and painful bodies, as well as shattered souls that no one can comprehend unless you've personally been there, like me and my angelic friend.

We've laughed and cried together, spent hours sharing each of our personal lifelong stories.

We both agree that our diseases have humbled us and are thankful to God for how he continually blesses us with his goodness and kindness.

As we both walk down our lonely roads together, although diseases different, we both experience such daily discomfort and pain.

Depression then sets in, and we just want all the suffering to end.

Only God knows when, but some days, it's so tough to trust, to keep our eyes fixed only on Him.

My angel in disguise is my friend, and no matter what happens, she won't be afraid to get involved with a sick friend and will always be there till the end.

I read God's prayers and inspiring poetry to her when she's down and hopeless.

She tells me how peaceful and calm the readings make her feel and how she can truly visualize every word, bringing her peace, calmness, and happiness that I know is God's will.

When I am afraid and in tears, she offers a prayer of comfort, especially for me, with God giving her the words that I need to hear.

I feel God is then speaking through her and telling me it will be *okay*.

"You're never alone.

Keep holding onto Me."

Telling her, through so many tears I have cried, "I just can't go on," and how I want to go home and be with God from this moment on.

She answers by softly stating to me:

"Honey, God's not ready for you. He's not finished with you yet.

When it's your time, He will come and take you to live with Him."

God sends us angels in disguise—to help us through our sorrows, pain, and unbearable suffering.

I love my friend because she's an encourager, gentle, and aways so kind.

Journeying down life's difficult road, our loving God sends special people to help us in our time of need.

God plants a small seed and nurtures it with His love and His great sovereignty.

He watches how it grows and blooms into a beautiful friendship between two friends that become so true and wise.

In her, God sends me an angel in disguise.

Our mighty Lord put us together many years ago as friends, knowing our lives would become intertwined years later, becoming best friends through each other's suffering.

We try to have faith through all of this but, many days, just can't see beyond the endless moments, minutes, and hours of tearful misery.

I pray to God to end this dark road of suffering and fears for both of us, acknowledging God—that in many ways, each of us is still blessed.

Sometimes, my special friend asks me to pray for her and I ask her to pray for me.

Other times, we pray together over the phone, knowing we have a direct connection with our mighty Lord, He who hears us and the one from whom all blessings flow.

He brings us peace and comfort for our weary souls, as well as rest for our bodies.

My friend and I are sisters by faith and sisters by heart.

I pray God will always be in the middle of our deep friendship and never let two fragile and caring hearts part.

Respect and understanding she and I have for one another, as we continually look to God the Father for help and strength, for there is no other.

Angels in disguise, sometimes we see them; other times, they are invisible from our eyes; but most times, God sends them to us in the form of a best friend who's consistently on our side.

My heart is broken when I hear how much suffering she's in— fear of living the way she must live the rest of her life without any end.

She always offers comforting words when she hears my cries and shattered dreams; that's why I call her my angel in disguise.

She has a heartfelt spirit of love and cares about everyone.

We've both had friends and family in our lives that have done us wrong, not able to accept our lives of disability.

Cruel words and actions hurt when there's a lack of understanding.

They have no idea how hard it is to fight daily with such intense physical pain, which then turns into unending emotional pain.

Hour after hour, day after day, watching sadly as life continues to pass us by.

When people don't understand a debilitating condition, they pull away, don't know what to say, but for us, it's just part of them leaving us behind.

My friend and I must learn to accept what they don't understand, praying for them that, one day, they eventually can.

We truly are grateful to God for our bond of friendship, choosing to journey together, along each other's path of personal suffering.

We both accept responsibility for a strong yet delicate friendship, having so many emotions attached to a constant illness.

My friend and I converse about heaven being such a beautiful healing place and how we'll see God's loving face and feel the radiance of His healing grace.

And should one of us die before the other, we'll eagerly await in heaven for the one that, on earth, was left behind.

One day, our friendship will be renewed and continue in heaven's most beautiful place.

We will both be healed, feeling such joy and peace.

Once again, we will be laughing, singing, and dancing, where all of our pain and suffering will finally and forever be released.

Some friends, you have for a little while, few all through a person's life; still, some just float through a small passing window of time.

Then one day, God sends another blessing—a special friend who understands, someone who is caring, compassionate, loving, and wise.

I will continually praise God for blessing me each and every day with my longtime friend who is constantly, no matter life's circumstance, always by my side.

In Lisa, God sends me my angel in disguise.

He died for us that, whether we are awake or asleep, we may live together with Him.

> *Therefore encourage one another and build each*
> *other up, just as, in fact, you are doing.*
> —1 Thessalonians 5:10–11

     PATRICIA ANNE "PATTI" MEITZLER DAVIS

The Joys of Heaven

A Prayer for Comfort and Peace

To my godfather, Bob Testerman

What is heaven?

Heaven is the most beautiful, peaceful place anyone can ever imagine.

Heaven is where Jesus and his angels live.

An earthly life, once filled with suffering, pain, and fears will be no more, as Jesus takes my hand and escorts me through heaven's most majestic doors.

Away from my sick and painful body, I'll be more alive and be forever by my Savior's side.

I won't ever suffer again or feel any pain because the love of Jesus will be enveloping me all around, and my ears will hear trumpets of angels filled with wondrous love resound.

Heaven is my one true home that's filled with beauty and peace like I've never ever known.

Jesus will welcome me home and wrap His loving arms around me.

My spirit will be filled with warmth, comfort, and unimaginable peace.

I'll never be alone or afraid again because Jesus paid the price for all my sins.

To me, heaven is a place where the beauty of sunsets never dim and the sun never fades, where God's radiant beams shine warmth each and every day.

There will always be laughter instead of sorrow,
joy instead of crying,
healing instead of sickness and pain.

Heaven will be filled with luminous beauty and love eternal.

Beautiful music with angels singing praises to God the Father, and glory to God in the highest will ring out in song.

Beautiful, vivid colors will align the heavens, like a painter uses his palette to paint dazzling rainbows and sunsets across the sky.

The air will be sweet and the waters exquisitely clear and pure.

Jesus shows me these things, then He takes my hand, and we continue our tour of my forever heaven homeland.

There will be fields of beautiful flowers and mountains of peace and serenity.

I will be reunited with all of my loved ones, and the angels will be rejoicing, then we will all dwell with the one true lamb who was slain for us—Jesus.

He will smile and say:

"Welcome home, my child, for even though I have always been with you, I saw on earth how you were suffering all the while, but now, you are free from your prison of pain and disease.

Take rest and find joy and comfort in Me and trust in My unconditional love. You are home now. Come live with Me in eternal peace in My beautiful kingdom of heaven."

For God so loved the world, that He gave His one and only son, that whoever believes in Him shall not perish but have eternal life.
—John 3:16

And if I go and prepare a place for you, I will
come back and take you to be with Me
that you also may be where I am.

—John 14:3

Jesus, My Friend

A Prayer of Peace and Comfort

Fields of colorful flowers underneath a majestic blue sky,
with pillow-soft clouds passing me by.

I gaze around and see a single rose, which reflects the amazing tenderness and unconditional love that our Lord shows,

but the thorns—a reminder of his crown, which was once so painfully worn.

Along with the beauty and life of this world, we are constantly reminded of pain, suffering, and death that we all must face.

Jesus gives us an eternal promise of heaven, that if we believe in Him and repent of our sin, he will take us to glorious heaven, that most beautiful place, where all will be healed and all will be made well.

We will dwell with our one true king, and endless praising we shall sing.

We must all travel down life's difficult path, where there are seasons for laughter, joy, pain, and suffering.

Our Lord never promised us an easy life, but He did promise we would never have to walk alone.

He promised to always be with us, showing unconditional love and giving us eternal peace and blessing, great mercy and compassion, which we have never truly known.

On my personal journey, Jesus meets and greets me on life's most difficult path.

He takes my hand and smiles, as He begins to walk beside me.

With one miraculous touch, Jesus heals instantly, restoring my broken body that the enemy had stolen from me.

My Lord shows me the world's glorious beauty, which includes God's innocent animals and nature's tall, soft, windblown trees.

Together, we climb the high majestic mountains, beholding all of God's creation as far as the eye can see.

He then parts the seas, and I hear angelic songs from the heavens proclaiming Jesus as Lord and His highest majesty.

Jesus then commands the storming winds to sing me a song of serenity.

We walk along a sun-drenched beach, our bare feet feeling the warm, sun-kissed sand.

My Lord turns to me and smiles as He reaches and clasps both of my hands and says:

"I'm not only your loving heavenly Father but also your unconditional friend, always loving and forgiving you time after time again.

Never be afraid, My child, to come to me about anything, for I will be with you in good times and even closer to you still in all of life's hardships of suffering."

My heart is filled with such gladness and great peace,
that to my Lord and Savior, my prayers will never cease.

Then he turns and smiles, showing me such deep, caring, and compassionate eyes that I know I'd be with him in heaven, should I suddenly die.

Jesus lovingly again speaks to me:

"You're My precious child, and I'm your need—and I'll always be with you and never ever leave.

No matter what trials you may have to endure in this life or sickness you may have to face, it is in My strong arms where you'll find sustained peace and everlasting grace."

As the calm winds gently sweep across the land, I know and think I'll never be alone because the Lord has my heart and He now has my hand.

In times of great suffering and unbearable pain, He will carry me in His arms and say:

"Don't be afraid and don't be scared, I have already paid the price to forgive your sins.

I will always love you and be with you because I am your heavenly Father and I am also Jesus, your friend."

> *Peace I leave with you; My peace I give you. I*
> *do not give to you as the world gives.*
> *Do not let your hearts be troubled and do not be afraid.*
> —John 14:27

Little Lamb Lost

An Inspiration of Suffering, Faith, and Comfort

When the burden of my suffering becomes too great and overwhelms me, my soul wants to escape my broken body and fly away to be with God in heaven above.

The pain I must endure seems so unreal, like a terrible dream that I cannot escape or awaken from.

Who does God choose to heal and why only some?

I wonder what God's purpose for my life is—even for my very existence.

As I struggle daily for an answer, all I can seem to hear is silence.

Why, Lord? Why me?

Once a gifted music teacher and Christian singer,

I used my singing voice to lift you up in beautiful song.

Through my physical limitations and so much discomfort and pain,

I now only have memories of the praises to You I continually once sang.

I ask, "How can I serve you like this, in this horribly painful condition?

Is there something in my terrible suffering that I fail to see but serves Your higher purpose or someone else in need?"

My whole life gone, never to be the same; some days, I want to find someone, anyone to blame.

I wander aimlessly around in pain, like a wounded, dying animal that separates itself willingly from its pack, my flesh falling victim to the enemy's constant attacks.

I am but a little lamb lost, seeking to be found, trying desperately to understand how pain and suffering can be part of your master plan.

Away from the world, alone and scared, searching for belonging in a place I don't recognize anymore.

I'm seeking my rescuer and healer, my constant shepherd, my Lord and Savior.

I long to follow You, listening for Your voice saying:

"Here I am, come to Me, my little lamb lost. Your shepherd am I, searching to bring you home. Come, follow, take My loving, strong hand.

You never have to be afraid or alone ever again, My little lamb lost."

Teach me, O Lord, to trust in You, even when I feel so lost, like a boat on a roaring, stormy sea that's being constantly thrown and tossed.

You, Lord, see our entire life and all of the trials and hardships we must endure and face.

You remind us of Your constant, loving presence in the midst of pain and tragedy, no matter how bad our days may become.

You offer unconditional forgiveness for making mistakes in choosing paths for ourselves that ultimately turn out wrong.

I trust and believe You want me to keep looking up, although hard and long are the days; the pain becomes continually persistent, wearing my body down and breaking my spirit.

What did I ever do to ultimately deserve such a terrible wrong?

I try to surround myself with Your presence: in written Word, uplifting stories, and programs, worship, praise, and meditating music, and constant prayers to You, oftentimes with tears streaming down my face.

I feel so lost as I search for peace, comfort, and Your loving grace.

You are my shepherd, and where You go, I want to follow.

At times, I feel so stranded and abandoned by everyone, not knowing which way to turn, hoping for direction from You, my shepherd; Your voice, may I learn.

Feeling like a small child, crying out in pain, wanting to crawl to You and sit upon Your lap, where You will wipe all the tears from my eyes.

With Your strong arms wrapped securely around me; your loving, gentle eyes will meet mine, and all the pain will forever be gone and left behind.

The constant daily physical sufferings make me feel I've lost my way, as I try to find you in something good each and every day.

As I wander and wander, the pain so agonizing, it drives me to fear:

"Where are You, my shepherd, are you really here?"

I am but a little lamb lost, seeking to be found, trying desperately to understand how pain and suffering can be part of your master plan.

Away from the world, alone and scared, searching for belonging in a place I don't recognize anymore.

I'm seeking my rescuer and healer, my constant shepherd, my Lord and Savior.

I long to follow You, listening for Your voice saying:

"Here I am, come to Me, my little lamb lost. Your shepherd am I, searching to bring you home. Come, follow, take My loving, strong hand.

You never have to be afraid or alone ever again, My little lamb lost."

Walking through this broken world, no one knows me.

I'm just another faceless person in a sea of so many, sharing shattered hopes and broken dreams, a person suffering intensely day after day; I may never know why.

Please forgive me, Jesus, for my sadness, all the tears, crying, and shameful complaining, for in my worst pain and discomfort do I find my faith waxing and waning.

My body thirsts for rest, comfort, and healing.

My soul seeks understanding, wisdom, strength, and perseverance that only You, my shepherd, can provide.

So many days, I've lost my way, not knowing how to cope or even how to survive.

I once felt like a beautiful, healthy flower that was happy and bloomed with such beauty and grace.

Now, with each passing day, I'm not sure what I will have to learn to endure or eventually face.

My painful body can no longer hide the damaging effects from the stress of my illness.

My once pretty flower petals are drying up, fading, and falling away.

When will my shepherd come find me and say:

"You've had enough. Come, follow, and be with Me this day"?

I never envisioned my life living like this, being struck by a debilitating illness at my age—being so painfully tough.

Giving up my singing career has cost me many unanswered questions, as I've shed lots of bitter, painful tears.

Relying on others to help me is difficult, when I used to be so independent; now, my affliction is so painful and emotionally rough.

I am so weary and want to lay down my cross and let the tears flow freely.

Not feeling I can withstand any more pain or negative feelings, still I pray to You, Jesus, for help and a miracle healing.

Please, my shepherd, how I long to hear You call my name—
your little lamb lost that once you bought at a painful cost.

I am but a little lamb lost, seeking to be found, trying desperately to understand how pain and suffering can be part of Your
master plan.

Away from the world, alone and scared, searching for belonging
in a place I don't recognize anymore.

I'm seeking my rescuer and healer, my constant shepherd, my
Lord and Savior.

I long to follow You, listening for Your voice saying:

"Here I am, come to Me, My little lamb lost. Your shepherd
am I, searching to bring you home. Come, follow, take My loving,
strong hand.

You never have to be afraid or alone ever again, My little lamb
lost."

My Lord recently called my dear sweet godfather home after
suffering a debilitating illness that was painful and helpless to watch.

I remember in those last weeks and days, sitting with him holding his hand.

I thanked and told him how grateful I was and how much I had
always loved him for being such a great second dad, as I kissed him
gently on his cheek and again on his forehead.

On one occasion of our precious time together, as he was near-
ing the end of his earthly life, he whispered to me how he wondered
what heaven was like.

We talked about this for a while, as I offered to read a special prayer that I had written especially for him, titled "The Joys of
Heaven."

I choked back the tears as I began to read slowly to him, making
sure the message and meaning of the words he could comprehend.

Afterward, he told me, "I liked it very much. Thank you for
writing it for me."

I started to cry as I softly told him in heaven, he'd be free to walk, run, laugh, and able to speak without so much difficulty.

I reassured him one day, all of us, his family, would be with him, and what a reunion it would be.

He seemed to be more at peace, as a calm came over him and his hand that I had been holding had stopped shaking uncontrollably, as I was seeing firsthand how terribly hard his suffering was and could be.

Another blessing he had given to me was when he quietly spoke of all the beautiful organ music he had been hearing and how it was all around and asked if I could hear it.

At that moment, I knew my sweet godfather was catching glimpses of the beauty of heaven.

He was another little lamb that Jesus, his shepherd, was preparing to gently call home.

In his last few days, as difficult as it was, I saw his frail and weakened body continue to decline; however, his soul remained strong as he struggled to hold on.

Like a newborn baby, he was completely dependent on others for his every basic physical need, as his body continued to shut down.

Again, I knew that the time was drawing near that Jesus, soon, would be calling my godfather, another one of His precious lambs, home.

At any moment, he would be forever at peace with his smiling and loving shepherd, never to suffer again or ever to feel alone.

When someone we love suffers and eventually passes on, it is a blessing for the one who has had to endure, but for family and friends left behind, they will undoubtedly feel great sadness and be ever so lost and completely heartbroken.

They may even question, "Why, Lord, why?" when all they really wanted was more time with their loved one and to have their lives restored to once what they had been.

We may take great comfort that Jesus, our perfect shepherd, knows all of us by name, whether we are alive or have already passed on.

To Him, we are all His little children, His sweet little lambs.

With so much forgiveness and compassion, He loves us all, but it may be hard to feel and comprehend when we suffer and the pain of our emotions can become overbearingly raw.

There are so many ways we, as imperfect human beings, may become little lambs lost.

Chronic pain and suffering, sickness, disease, unbearable grief, frustration, loneliness, isolation, loss of friendships and family, abandonment, divorce, abuse, depression, anxiety, anger, fear, and death of loved ones.

For me personally, I have experienced every single one of the above, but I rejoice in my shepherd's forgiveness, understanding, and unconditional love.

He sustains me with strength and with hope when, most days, I can barely cope.

With the loss of my old life on this earth due to my failing health, I must remember Jesus, my shepherd, sacrificed His life for mine.

He was the one true lamb who was slain.

On His beaten, bloody, and bruised shoulders, He carried the burden of all mankind's sin, as He took the whole world's blame so we would not have to live according to our shame.

Through oceans of tears, I still continue to pray and cry out to Him,

for divine healing and restoration of my body to the way I once had been.

I know He still performs miracles and believe in my heart that He truly can.

I tell Him I feel so lost, to please be my shepherd, to guide His little lamb lost out of the pain and darkness of despair, which, on many days, cloud my judgment, making it difficult to see and to even think clear.

On a difficult road so dark, my shepherd lights the way, taking my hand and saying:

"Come, little lamb, and be with Me this day and for all eternity."

I am but a little lamb lost, seeking to be found, trying desperately to understand how pain and suffering can be part of your master plan.

Away from the world, alone and scared, searching for belonging in a place I don't recognize anymore.

I'm seeking my rescuer and healer, my constant shepherd, my Lord and Savior.

I long to follow You, listening for Your voice saying:

"Here I am, come to Me, my little lamb lost. Your shepherd am I, searching to bring you home. Come, follow, take My loving, strong hand.

You never have to be afraid or alone ever again, My little lamb lost."

I will continue to follow You, my shepherd, despite what I may have to endure or what this broken world may bring.

Through daily prayer, I ask You to strengthen and lead me, Your little lamb lost.

Please, Lord, help me not to go astray, constantly lifting me up into Your presence each and every day.

Following Your voice, I'll listen and do my best to always obey.

One day, my turn will come, where my shepherd will be calling me home, and I will say:

"Here I am. Please come take me home, Lord, for in this troubled world of suffering, sickness, tragedy, and pain, I've always been Your little lost lamb."

My sheep listen to My voice; I know them and they follow Me.
I give them eternal life, and they shall never perish;
no one can snatch them out of My hand.
—John 10:27–28

# Jesus, Close to My Heart

A Prayer of Suffering, Hope, and Renewed Strength

The blessings of this world are not always easy to see, as our life may not turn out as we intended it to be.

Acceptance is difficult when someone's life is filled with pain and tragedy.

Please, Jesus, open my eyes so they may focus on You and clearly see all the many blessings You have bestowed upon me.

Help me to recognize when You're speaking to me, guiding my mind and heart to stop and listen when You say, "Be still and know that I am God" (Psalm 46:10).

When I am in the darkest valley of my darkest hour, help me to know Your ever constant presence is with me by showing Your great unconditional love, helping me to believe.

No matter the pain my body suffers, my soul belongs to You.

A humble servant, I strive to be, acknowledging that You are my one true and only need.

My spirit wants to take flight and longs to break free, soaring to heaven, where I know You, my Lord, will be.

Jesus, please stay close to my heart—in constant suffering, when I'm falling apart.

Help me to know You are with me when I don't understand, feel abandoned, and just can't see.

Tears falling to the ground like an endless waterfall,

You, Jesus, are the one to whom I shall pray and always shall call.

Your mercy is great with Your love abounding strong, as I lift praises to You in resounding song.

You died for me to set my soul free;

thank You for my growing relationship with You and for my eyes with which to see.

Never shall You leave me, never shall You part;

Jesus, please stay close to my heart.

Help me to inspire people and to do Your will, listening for Your loving voice when mine won't be still.

Please calm the fears and dry all my tears, taking away not only my pain and suffering but also the depression and unwanted negativity I constantly struggle with each and every day.

I desire to be with You, Jesus, above all else, as I realize that every worldly thing falls away then dies and eventually decays, but the love and faith of You, Lord, is everlasting and eternal.

Like a winged eagle soaring freely through the sky, looking down on God's beautiful earth as it continues to fly, my soul longs to be free from my painful shell, ascending to You, Jesus, my creator, where I won't be sick or feel pain anymore.

My one and only prayer is to be healed and to be forever with You, Lord, in heaven, where I know I'll always be well.

I cry out to You, O Lord, from the deepest depths within my soul. Please hear my cries in heaven above, from Your weary child on earth below, who is suffering so, desiring Your great mercy and ever comforting love.

Please be near and offer serenity to my broken and worn body.

Feed my tired soul with Your strength, hope, and compassion.

Help me with my spiritual growth, although my flesh is painfully weak; it is You, Lord, that my soul continually seeks.

Jesus, please stay close to my heart—in constant suffering, when I'm falling apart.

Help me to know You are with me when I don't understand, feel abandoned, and just can't see.

Tears falling to the ground like an endless waterfall,

You, Jesus, are the one to whom I shall pray and always shall call.

Your mercy is great with Your love abounding strong, as I lift praises to You in resounding song.

You died for me to set my soul free;

thank You for my growing relationship with You and for my eyes with which to see.

Never shall You leave me, never shall You part;

Jesus, please stay close to my heart.

I pray healing for all the sick, dying, and afflicted around the world, people of all ages and of all races, unimaginable suffering in so many ways that people globally must endure and face every single day.

Life can be ever so cruel and unfair for many to live, causing us to become so discouraged and even question where God is.

It's so easy to develop anger and bitterness when we are faced with illness or disease that causes indescribable pain and suffering.

A poisonous vine that takes root and starts to grow—eventually, it wraps around our heart, choking all the life and goodness out of us that once we did know.

These vicious weeds must be stopped, ripped out, and torn apart.

I pray Jesus will remove and replace all the destructive vines with healthy, beautiful, blossoming flowers of hope and love, and may His mercy shine, while whispering into our suffering bodies and broken hearts, "Peace be thine."

I come before You in prayer, Jesus, while suffering with constant tormenting pain that is both physically and emotionally tough. Please keep me a humble person, remembering to pray for other's needs. Please do not allow me to become a destructive weed; guide me in sowing only good seeds.

When my days become so overwhelming with pain, do not let me wander far from You but continue in following Your lead.

Help me to show You thanksgiving and praise and to serve You, even if it's just in some small, simple way, as I continue to live with constant chronic pain, frustration, anger, and severe sadness followed by crying fits set in;

I realize these emotions are all part of my human suffering and the grieving process of my wonderful life that once had been.

The loss of dear friends and some family makes me so sad, especially when I recall all of the wonderful memories we all did have over the years before I became ill.

They chose to leave me because they couldn't begin to understand the sufferings of my painfully difficult life, like a beautiful, calm sea turning stormy, causing enormous waves of strife.

I pray to my Lord not to let a poisonous vine take hold of my heart, but compassion and forgiveness, I hope to find.

The suffering patient needs constant support and understanding from people who truly care, who do not display judgmental attitudes. They also need people who are willing to give all kinds of physical and emotional help, displaying a genuine love for people in need, which requires time, patience, and sacrifice, just as Jesus did when He was willingly crucified.

I pray for the friends I once had but now have lost, that the Lord might touch their hearts and minds with the wisdom of understanding in showing empathy for others, when suffering consumes a person's life—my life, their once devoted friend.

Maybe one day, the Lord will have our paths cross again, thus bringing healing to me as well as to them.

Remembering all the fun we used to have and all the plans we used to make now just brings tears to my eyes, for it's just another devastating loss that I cannot control due to the world's ignorance and lack of understanding toward the chronically ill.

Jesus, please stay close to my heart—in constant suffering, when I'm falling apart.

Help me to know You are with me when I don't understand, feel abandoned, and just can't see.

Tears falling to the ground like an endless waterfall,

You, Jesus, are the one to whom I shall pray and always shall call.

Your mercy is great with Your love abounding strong, as I lift praises to You in resounding song.

You died for me to set my soul free;

thank You for my growing relationship with You and for my eyes with which to see.

Never shall You leave me, never shall You part;

Jesus, please stay close to my heart.

I pray for Jesus to grant me peace each and every painful day and to also lead me down the road of righteousness. Severe trials and adversities can test our faith, make us stronger, and strengthen our character.

I pray to you, Lord, that my affliction does not make me become bitter or harden my heart.

I ask Jesus, please be near to my side and always let your love in me abide, especially when I'm falling apart, crying because I can't escape the pain and all the rest of my body hurts.

Thank You for my growing relationship with You, and in my prayers, I ask for my body and mind to be renewed daily and to be kept close to You.

Never shall You leave me, never shall You part;

thank You, Jesus, for staying so close to my heart.

Comforting Savior

A Prayer of Suffering, Comfort, and Encouragement

When the storms of life come upon me,
I have nowhere I can run and hide.
As I seek refuge in my perfect Savior, You, dear Lord, protect me, as a parent shelters their child from all harm and danger.
You were born as an innocent and holy child, coming into this broken and sinful world.
You didn't even have a bed,
only a lowly manger in which to lay Your sweet head.
You grew into a man, humble, compassionate, and loving,
speaking only God's truth all of the time,
healing the brokenhearted and the sick; people from everywhere flocked to see You because You were so patient and so kind.

As a human being, You experienced the worst pain and suffering known to mankind.
You willingly died a horribly painful death, as You chose to carry out Your Father's will, which was already set.
You became God's sacrificial lamb for all the world to see.
From upon the cross, You made Your one painful and agonizing plea:
"Father, why hast Thou forsaken me?"
Always selfless and blameless, never knowing sin, for You were God's greatest gift to the world, the perfect Son of Man.

You, my Savior, know what each and every one of us on this earth is going through because You were once human too. Taking upon Yourself all our blame, You experienced such agonizing and tormenting pain, all the while feeling every positive and negative emotion a person could feel. Suffering so unjustly with physical and mental humiliation in unbearable pain, still You chose to endure and forgive, while people mocked, persecuted, and ultimately killed You.

Comforting Savior, I humbly pray to You;
Your divine mercy and favor I seek from this unbearable pain I'm walking through.
You understand the depth of my suffering, as You once suffered too.
Please hold me tenderly when I start to cry and forgive me when I beg to please just let me die.
Hold my hand and carry me when I no longer feel I can go on and uplift my broken spirit with Your encouraging word and beautiful song.
Calm my thoughts when they become out of control and send quickly your angels so to You, in heaven, they may carry my soul.
Help strengthen my faith when it constantly wavers, for I desperately need You, my comforting Savior.

I want to step out of the darkness, where my illness has cost me to lose my way, and walk into Your loving presence, the light of peace;
there, I'll be made whole, and all my suffering will cease.
Please teach me to have more faith, for I feel it is so weak.
Help me to solely rely upon You when my days are overwhelmingly too painful to endure and go through.
Many days, I cry and feel so scared and just can't seem to shake my fear.
Your voice I desperately want to hear, and Your calming presence I long to feel ever so near.

My suffering and pain feel like I'm a prisoner on a runaway train, hopelessly out of control, ready to run off a cliff and plunge straight into the pit.

Please ease my suffering even by a bit and take control of my life, granting me peace that things will be all right.

Please stop this runaway train of insurmountable suffering and pain that I can do nothing about.

Precious Savior, please take care of me in my time of need and stop the rivers of doubt that freely flow through my mind,

for it is Your great compassion and comfort that I seek to find.

I desire to be healed and for my heart to be filled with Your loving kindness and grace.

I ask for mercy and forgiveness for the ways my suffering causes me to behave.

A victim of illness and pain, as a result of living in a fallen world filled with sin.

I do not like the person I've become, as I cry and whine, feeling no better than a prisoner or a slave.

Please do not turn Your face from me but love and embrace me right where I am—in this storm of tribulation.

Comforting Savior, I humbly pray to You;

Your divine mercy and favor I seek from this unbearable pain I'm walking through.

You understand the depth of my suffering, as You once suffered too.

Please hold me tenderly when I start to cry and forgive me when I beg You to please just let me die.

Hold my hand and carry me when I no longer feel I can go on and uplift my broken spirit with Your encouraging word and beautiful song.

Calm my thoughts when they become out of control and send quickly your angels so to You, in heaven, they may carry my soul.

Help strengthen my faith when it constantly wavers, for I desperately need You, my comforting Savior.

Often, I think and dream of the glories of heaven, that wonderfully beautiful realm we cannot see but is promised to us and is waiting for all who believe.

Suffering and pain will always be a part of this world, and journeying through this life is but a moment in time.

Walking on life's uncertain road to our one true home—heaven—is a path which only shall we find through our comforting Savior, who is so loving and ever so kind.

Through His own human suffering and pain, He listens and understands us better than anyone can. He will always show us great compassion and mercy and a deep willingness to forgive all our sins.

As I lay down at night, I pray to You, Jesus, my Savior, that you'll command your angels to watch over me, protecting and keeping me while I sleep.

Please help my painful body to rest and quiet my mind from all fears.

When my tears fall gently on my pillow, please be near, while holding my hand, and forgive all my human failures and transgressions, while loving me still.

Jesus, it is only You that I long for and desperately need, as I call out to You to hear my plea.

Please hold me tenderly when I start to cry and forgive me when I cry out to You to just let me die.

Hold my hand and carry me when I feel I can't go on and uplift my broken spirit with Your encouraging word and beautiful song.

Calm my thoughts when they become out of control and send quickly your angels so to You, in heaven, they may carry my soul.

Help strengthen my faith when it constantly wavers, for I desperately need You, my loving, comforting Savior.

Prisms of Love

A Prayer of Suffering, Hope, Comfort, and Faith

Each one of us in this world has our own struggles, hardships, and many trials that we must face. No two people will ever have the same story, even the harshest of suffering God can use for His glory. Disease, pain, and chronic debilitating illness can leave us angry, confused, weak, and vulnerable. When we don't know what to do, we cry rivers of emotional tears, not wanting to fight anymore or continue to go on.

> *His strength is made perfect in our weakness.*
> —2 Corinthians 12:10

Each of us plays an integral part in God's master plan, even though we may never see, fully comprehend, or ever understand it.

Think of a beautiful, colorful quilt; each color and pattern is different and unique, yet it is only a small part of the whole large quilt in its entirety.

The colors and patterns touch each other on all sides, are carefully interwoven, and each has a purpose in making it complete.

When finished, the quilt is a beautiful multicolor masterpiece for the eyes to behold.

We can relate this same scenario to our lives.

Every single person on this earth, God makes individually exceptional.

He blesses each of us with special gifts, talents, and abilities. Sadly, for some of us, these gifts are mixed with our own painful personal stories of ongoing tragic suffering.

Just like the beautiful colors in the quilt, the stories of our personal lives and of our suffering are individual and truly unique. We all belong to a higher calling than just to ourselves, as we are all interwoven, connected, and touch others with our own distinct stories.

Just the essence of our being, of who we are, is important because we are here, we are living now, and each of us touches and impacts other people throughout our lives. We may never know who, when, or how we reach others, but God does because he made us all part of his beautiful human quilt. He sees the big picture, even when we cannot. We are all so special as children of God, as He comforts those in their most distressing hour, for He is the God of unconditional love.

No matter what anyone's circumstance, whether it be good or bad, we are all part of the beautiful, colorful quilt that God continues to weave. We all will, or have already in some way, touched someone else's life, for we are all human and our lives truly intertwine with others in ways we may never ever know, for only our loving God is in control.

One of the most precious gifts that God gives to each of us is our tears.

People cry for many different reasons and for many lengths of time.

Tears of joy and happiness, tears of sorrow and sadness, tears cried through continued pain and suffering, or tears shed over a long-time emotional wound, such as the loss of a loved one.

Because of my physical pain and the destruction and toll it takes on my body, I cry at least once every day, calling out to God for strength to endure and to please help me.

Still grieving the person I once was, I'm having much difficulty accepting my great loss.

One of my favorite sayings in the Bible comes from Psalm 56:8:

> *You keep track of all my sorrows.*
> *You have collected all my tears in your bottle.*
> *You have recorded each one in your book.*

I believe that Father God loves us so much, even more so when we are suffering afflictions, battling and struggling with anything that causes us to cry out to Him with beautiful, pure, and honest tears. They flow from the innermost and deepest part of our heart and our soul. God cares for us deeply, feels our pain, and sees our tears as they overflow.

I find it very comforting to know God is so merciful and compassionate, keeping track of all of our sorrows, collecting each tear that we cry, then keeping a record of it all.

How thankful and grateful I am for what our Lord and Savior does for us.

Our tears are prisms of love—
each one unique and rare, a gift from God in heaven above.
Reflections of cries to our Lord in joy or in our suffering—
each tear that we shed holds a key to unlock our heartfelt emotions.

Are we happy, filled with joy, sadness, sorrow, or in severe pain from our suffering?

When we cry for ourselves or for others, consider your tears prisms of love—

That are sent to the Father above.

He wants to comfort us, as His children we are.

He's close to the brokenhearted and sick, to the hopeless, dying, and suffering.

He's nearer to us than we can possibly believe.

Our tears (prisms) are all connected in God's beautiful, colorful human quilt that He continues to weave.

A cleansing for our spirit when tears start to fall, refracting light, like beautiful, glistening dewdrops.

Each one running down our cheeks, coming from our eyes—the windows to the light within our broken soul.

As we pray and cry openly and honestly with our loving Father in heaven above,

always remember, your beautifully painful tears are prisms of love.

Prisms can be seen in many vibrant colors that make up a beautiful rainbow across a clouded sky, refracting light back, bringing into focus God's beautiful colors and His wonderful promises to our sight. Stunning, gorgeous prisms in the form of a colorful rainbow at the bottom of a majestic white waterfall, I have seen. The thunderous rushing of water and uprising of cooling mist reminds me of God's magnificent power and unspoiled beauty that only comes from our Father in heaven above.

For me, the most beautiful prisms are the heartfelt tears of suffering that we shed.

Each one unique, no two ever alike, similar to beautiful, icy snowflakes sparkling down on a dark winter's night. Each white flake has its own pattern and shape, falling softly to the ground without a sound.

Our tears, crystal droplets raining down, belonging to a special person, their own individual story told behind each one, similar to writing a melodious song that's never been sung.

Like the beautiful multicolor-patterned quilt, we are all connected. Our tears are all different, but each person sheds them for their own special reasons and in different seasons of their life. They all have great meaning and importance to our creator, Father God.

We are all part of a human sea of tears, crying out in need to our heavenly Lord above.

Reflections of our deepest emotions never go unnoticed by our unconditional, loving, and compassionate God, who, in His mercy, unfailingly sees your tears, your prisms of love.

Our tears are prisms of love—
each one unique and rare, a gift from God in heaven above.
Reflections of cries to our Lord in joy or in our suffering—
each tear that we shed holds a key to unlock our heartfelt emotions.
Are we happy, filled with joy, sadness, sorrow, or in severe pain from our suffering?
When we cry for ourselves or for others, consider your tears prisms of love—
that are sent to the Father above.
He wants to comfort us, as His children we are.
He's close to the brokenhearted and sick, to the hopeless, dying, and suffering.
He's nearer to us than we can possibly believe.
Our tears (prisms) are all connected in God's beautiful, colorful human quilt that He continues to weave.
A cleansing for our spirit when tears start to fall, refracting light, like beautiful, glistening dewdrops.
Each one running down our cheeks, coming from our eyes— the windows to the light within our broken soul.
As we pray and cry openly and honestly with our loving Father in heaven above,
always remember, your beautifully painful tears are prisms of love,
and God will take mercy and honor you with His peaceful presence and comforting love.

Blessed are those who mourn, for they will be comforted.
—Matthew 5:4

Prayers, Sealed with Falling Tears

A Prayer of Suffering, Endurance, and Hope

In the stillness of the night, I pray to you, O Lord, for healing, as my body and soul are broken from the inside out.

Searching for a ray of hope and sunshine, when my body is in pain and when my spirit feels trapped and is filled with unwanted despair and doubt.

Dear Lord, Your will I wish to do, but my illness and constant pain—a daily thorn which humbly reminds me I can do nothing apart from You.

My weary body is tired of this physical pain and suffering, and my eyes, which are so swollen with tears, want to close and just sleep; alone, by myself, You, Jesus, are the one that hears and sees the bitter sad painful tears that I weep.

Please, Lord, come and find me, for I feel like that one lost sheep that wandered away because I can't bear to face another day.

I pray to You, Jesus, healer of broken bodies, keeper of fragile hearts and weary souls. Please, to my side, draw near, for these are my prayers, sealed with falling tears.

Like a piece of lonely driftwood floating in the soft waves of the sea, so my life is drifting through space and time, watching helplessly as life goes on for everyone.

As the seasons change, I remain the same, still battling, struggling, and fighting with destructive pain. I feel cut off from family events because I never feel well enough to attend. They don't know what to do or say, except I'm ever so grateful that they tell me that they continue to pray.

Please, Jesus, come and make me new, as I pray for a divine healing that can only come from You.

This war my body is rebelling from is wearing me down physically, emotionally, and spiritually. I feel like I'm beginning to drown, like two silent ships passing in the night that are on a collision course, sinking slowly and starting to go down.

My soul and painful body need to be lifted up by You, O Lord, and granted a healing which would be ever so profound.

I'm constantly thinking and meditating upon beautiful heaven and being there with You, my Lord, all the time. I pray and wonder how long it will be until I see You and feel Your welcoming embrace.

Jesus, it's You I pray to see, to gaze into Your deep, loving, peaceful eyes and to behold the radiant glow of Your unconditional, loving holy face.

I trust and believe You understand my every fear, for only You, Lord, know the many depths of each and every one of my painful tears.

I pray to You, Jesus, healer of broken bodies, keeper of fragile hearts and weary souls. Please, to my side, draw near, for these are my prayers, sealed with falling tears.

As dewdrops form in the coolness of the night, so fall my tears sparkling in the moonlight. I long for You, my Lord, of coming home to the beauty and peacefulness of heaven, where You'll be there waiting for me, smiling.

You are so pure and holy, Lord; help me in my human frailty to be more thankful and to honor You with worship and praise, which I know You truly deserve.

My prayer is, one day, You will have a place in heaven for me already reserved.

With all Your heavenly angels, I'll once again be able to sing, bringing You honor and glory, and all of heaven will join in proclaiming You, Jesus, as Savior and king, and I will be able to truly smile with joy again.

What a celebration we will have with our glorious Savior!

Reunions of friends and family, whom we once mourned, will be joining us in celebration of song, worship, and praise.

Happiness and joyful hearts will fill our perfect days, as we commune and fellowship with Jesus, our one true heavenly king.

I pray all my prayers will come to pass, for this world is not the one that will last. My need for You, Jesus, is great; please forgive all my sins of the past and grant me in having a relationship with You— the only one which will forever last.

Please allow me to feel Your presence when my days become too painful to endure.

Do not let me close the door to my life but yield to me Your sustaining peace—that You are always with me. May your unconditional love, I will feel always and forevermore.

I pray to You, Jesus, healer of broken bodies, keeper of fragile hearts and weary souls. Please, to my side, draw near, for these are my prayers, sealed with falling tears.

One day, my prayers will be answered and my suffering will be over, even if not in this life or world—then in heaven, where there will be abounding love, joy, and healing.

There I'll be forever free from my pain and illness and able to spend every beautiful day with Jesus, my healing Savior in eternity.

I imagine what a conversation that would be—between Jesus and me.

In heaven, Jesus says, "I heard every prayer, counted and saved every tear from all your lifelong sufferings. I was constantly with you, even in the darkest storms of life, and I never left your side, even through some of the worst trials you ever had to face."

I then ask him, "Where were You when I couldn't feel your presence, was so lonely, and could feel only pain?"

Jesus answers, "I was always with you, my lost little one, and never left your side, not once. I know that because of your pain, you felt abandoned and lonely, but I never forsake or leave My children, for I am with them always and closest to them in their times of trials and trouble, sickness, and disease.

All you have to do is lean on Me, talk to Me, and pray for what you need, for I love and comfort unconditionally all those who call upon me."

Suddenly in heaven, I fall before Jesus on my knees, giving Him thanksgiving and praise for His constant believing in me, even when I was too hurt, angry, or in so much pain, I just couldn't see. I said "Thank You" to Him for loving me all through my life unconditionally, even when the most negative storms kept knocking me down flat to the ground. "I couldn't have made it if You, Jesus, wouldn't have been there to lift me up."

Expressing to Jesus I have a special prayer I'd like to share with Him, lovingly, He agrees, as He smiles and sits patiently. He listens to my heartfelt prayer reflecting thankfulness and how good my Lord has been to me over the years, even when I failed to see. You always forgave and took me back willingly—

I thank You, Jesus, for healing my broken body and keeping my fragile heart and weary soul from harm. Thank You, precious Savior, for coming to my side and drawing ever so near to me. You heard and answered my prayers, while You counted and received all my lifelong tears of suffering. You released them into heaven, where they turned into sparkling drops of joy and praise. For it is only You, Lord, that can turn mourning and sorrow into joy and praise. You make everything so wonderfully and happily new, not just for a few but for everyone who believes in and accepts You.

As Jesus starts to walk toward me, He smiles, takes my hands, and states, "In heaven, there will never be any more prayers sealed with falling tears. You are home with Me now, are completely healed, and I will love you my child for all eternity."

> *You keep track of all my sorrows.*
> *You have collected all my tears in your bottle.*
> *You have recorded each one in your book.*
> —Psalm 56:8

> *You are forgiving and good, O Lord, abounding*
> *in love to all who call on You.*
> *Hear my prayer, O Lord; listen to my cry for mercy.*
> *In the day of my trouble, I will call to You, for You will answer me.*
> —Psalm 86:5–7

Gifts of Beauty and Meaning in Suffering at Christmastime

A Christmas Story of Forgiveness, Healing, Grace, Compassion, and Love

As my tired, sick body becomes so worn down, fighting with chronic debilitating pain, the burden of living becomes almost intolerable, making life difficult to live, not wanting to go on. I realize this is how my dad felt living and dying with chronic illness.

My thoughts, prayers, hopes, and dreams turn toward heaven, where Jesus is and where my dad now lives. It's a place where I believe I'll see all my loved ones again, where all pain and suffering will be forever gone. The beauty of our Lord and Savior will shine with unconditional love, radiance, and pure warmth, as He welcomes each one of us by name from this long, painful journey on earth into our perfect heavenly home.

As the holidays approach, Christmas for many people is a joyous celebration consisting of festive parties, decadent food, material gifts, and spending happy times with family and friends. For many others, like myself, it is a time for great sadness, loss, and pain.

My dad died at Christmastime after a long battle with a terrible sickness and disease. I remember those events, like it was yesterday; that painful year, I will never forget. It was filled with many blessings yet mixed with sad regrets. My grandmamma insisted we all come together as a family for Christmas, despite just burying her only son, my dad, just three days before. Dinner was painfully strained, as we all struggled to find our way and make any sense out of that holiday. The silence around the table was deafening, and afterward, as we all gathered, no one knew what to say, and gifts just didn't seem appropriate that mournful Christmas Day. It was a terribly sad time in my life and a tragic, heartbreaking Christmas that changed everyone in my family. My one consoling thought was that I knew Dad wasn't suffering anymore. Still, it was difficult for me, looking at his Christmas gift that I had bought for him, knowing he would never get to wear them, and thinking how hard it was going to be trying to celebrate Christmas at his mom's without him being there. Looking back, I realized my grandmamma wanted her family around her that year because of her own intense grief, which she never shared. She was one of the most strong-willed and stoic women I had ever known, never capable of outwardly showing sadness or negative emotions, although, in some way, we are all broken.

I was with my grandmamma that day when the doctor came out and told her there was nothing more to be done for her son. He continued by stating that because of the severity and toll the illness had taken on my dad's body (who was in his early fifties), he was living in a decaying shell dying, similar to a sick person who was in their eighties or nineties. He wouldn't even have survived a surgery he needed. I watched my grandmamma as she sat there completely silent, listening to the doctor's stinging words. She couldn't speak or shed any tears; it was as if she was in shock and a state of disbelief. She understood those fatal words of the doctor, as I knew her well enough to see pain and helplessness written all over her face, yet not once did she complain or ever want to talk about it. No parent should ever have to bury a child, yet it happens often, and many people are not aware of the horrific suffering others have the unfortunate burden to bear. I prayed to God that he wouldn't allow my dad to continue to suffer, even if it meant going home to Jesus and spending Christmas in heaven with Him there.

I had many issues with my dad while growing up, and at one point, we became estranged for several years. However, our gracious Lord granted me two years with my dad to reconcile—to try and make things right. I wasn't aware, at that time, these were to be the last two years of my dad's life. We spent time together rebuilding our severely broken relationship of a lifetime. He expressed how truly sorry he was to me and to our family for all of the mean and unkind things he had said and had done and for all the mistakes he kept repeating that hurt everyone. I, too, apologized for the things I had done and said out of hurt and anger. He explained to me that after all the horrible things he'd done, he never thought he would deserve to ever see me or his family again. He also told me he felt he didn't deserve to even have a daughter and asked how I could ever find it in my heart to truly forgive him.

Rewinding my story before all this took place, that first hospital visit—I had heard my dad was in the hospital and wasn't really expected to live. As I started to make my way to see him, after years of no communication, I suddenly lost my nerve, didn't think I could do it, and started to turn around and walk out. However, our loving God had other plans for me. God in His mercy, who forgives and always knows best, gave me the will, strength, and compassion to stop and not walk out of that hospital but to turn back around and continue walking directly into my dad's hospital room so unexpectedly.

Daddy was completely shocked to see me, as I started to ask how he was feeling. I told him I had been thinking a lot about the importance and meaning of life. In that very moment, I had made a conscious decision to give him my full forgiveness.

He was able and thankful to receive it, just as he embraced my sincere apologies for why I behaved out of hurtful, angry emotional reactions to what he had done. He told me he understood I was reacting the only way I knew how after he had hurt me and our family so deeply. This was our first of many healing, forgiving, and compassionate moments right there in his hospital room—a gift from God. He did recover enough to be let out of the hospital that time. This became a turning point in my life, not only with my dad but with my relationship with the Lord. I never would have thought anything like this would ever be possible, and I know my dad never thought so either because of the words he said to me that I already shared and wrote about earlier in my story. We serve a God of possibilities—

Things which are not possible with man are possible with God.
—Luke 18:27

I thanked God for the beautiful healing time He allowed me to have with my dad. In those last couple of years, I learned more about him, his feelings, and the depth of his sad, emotional pain. I had never seen this side of him, as he told me things I had never known before. I started to begin to understand why things happened and turned out the way that they did. Nothing was left unsaid between us, as we recalled some good times, but mainly the difficult ones. We both expressed the I'm sorrys, the I love yous, and, more importantly, the I forgive yous.

The day before he died, so close to Christmas, I sat by his hospital bed, holding his hand. He could hear me but could not speak; as he squeezed my hand to yes and no questions that I was asking him, I knew that he understood me. My dad had lived a very sad, emotionally painful life, and it just continued to get worse as he struggled with his physical disease. He was in and out of the hospital those last two years, and many times, I never knew if he'd be coming home again or not. Relationships in the family were strained and damaged, and no one really knew what to say or even how to accept him in the condition he was in. Disease and sickness can be such a lonely and painful road one must travel on. As I watched my daddy lie there, dying in that hospital bed, at times, I was overcome with grief, realizing but wondering why things had to turn out the way they did. The lost years he and I had, so much anger and bitterness, was all gone.

God had given me the grace and compassion to forgive, but how I wished he could have lived. One of my greatest gifts from God was being able to reconcile and have those two last years with him. Still, I felt so helpless watching him and holding his hand. We really do not know how truly fragile and valuable a human life is until we experience suffering or watch someone we love dying. For me, I gained perspective and insight into some of my own emotions. Forgiveness is a choice, and I am so grateful my dad and I could receive it before it was too late. Sitting there, my heart filled with grief; at the same time, God gave me peace knowing that over the last two years, I had brought my dad some joy, peace, forgiveness, and understanding, and he had done the same for me.

On his last night in the hospital, just days before Christmas, something remarkable happened. All of our family came in and gathered around his bed. I could hardly believe it myself, but here everyone was. My dad became more alert than he had been all day. He opened his eyes and sat up with help from the nurse. He was completely coherent and was able to speak and smile a little on that last evening of his life. He was like a dim candle that suddenly becomes bright and flickers one last time before it goes out. Daddy recognized everyone there, as he turned and gazed at each and every single one of us. He now knew he was not going to die alone. He had all of his family gathered around—all of us together in his hospital room. I knew this made him happy and brought him peace, everyone putting their differences aside to come together for him, despite all the problems of the past.

I considered this a Christmas miracle and God's will. These were the Lord's special Christmas gifts for me and my dad—forgiveness and healing, grace, compassion, and love. God placed a knowing upon my heart that night—it was to be the last time I would see

Daddy alive. Within hours of that entire family gathering, he was able to let go and pass peacefully. I knew he had died knowing that his family did care and that I loved and forgave him. There was this awesome sense of peace in my spirit that I felt could only have come from our heavenly Father above. As sad as it was that his passing was within days of Christmas, I knew his physical and emotional torment was over. God had heard my prayer and honored my wish about not letting his suffering continue, even if it meant my dad had to leave us all at Christmastime.

Sickness, disease, and chronic pain can all cause people to act and behave in ways that no one could possibly imagine unless they have experienced it themselves or have seen how it affects someone close to them. Even then, no one should ever compare an individual's pain and suffering to someone else's pain and suffering. We are all individuals, and what one person can tolerate, someone else may not be able to cope or withstand. A sick person's actions or words can, a lot of times, push friends and family members away. I watched this happen to my dad, and I even participated in it before I knew better. Now that I'm sick, I have even a greater understanding of how my poor daddy felt. I've lost friends, and people have stopped calling. When you live with a chronic debilitating disease, people don't understand. Friends and family that were once close just fade away; they don't know what to say, so it's much easier to walk away. The last two years of Daddy's health just continued to spiral downward, and it was hard sometimes for me to be with him, watching him suffer. He needed a friend, and he needed his daughter, and I was not going to let anything else come between us. I believed in my heart God wanted to fix our broken relationship and wanted me with my dad until the bitter end. Chronic disease and pain not only devastate the patient but everyone around them. The Bible states:

Judge not, and ye shall not be judged:
Condemn not, and ye shall not be condemned:
Forgive, and ye shall be forgiven:
—Luke 6:37

When I started to really listen to the gut-wrenching emotional pain Dad had long suffered, I stopped being mad and judgmental with him, being blinded for too many years with anger and resentment. I actually learned much about him and how sad his life had truly been. He explained to me why he could never cry but only once in his entire life. I genuinely felt real compassion for him—for everything he'd been through and for all the wrongs he had to endure throughout his life. God gave me wisdom and patience, along with sincere compassion and understanding, those final two years of his life. I believe God looks deep into a person's heart and sees and knows every intricate detail of their life circumstances. Our Lord Jesus is the only one who knows how and to what degree a person is suffering and why they may act or say things in such a way that may be offensive to others or even to God himself.

We serve a very forgiving Lord, and he has great mercy and compassion for all his children. He understands illness, pain, disease, death and dying, and the effects it can have on a person's mind, as well as to their physical body. Even though his health continued to fail, Daddy and I did more living and positive communicating over those final two years before he died than we had done in both of our entire lives. I fully credit our loving Father in heaven for this. God in His divine mercy brought two fragile, angry, damaged, and hurting sinners together in both me and my dad. God then blessed us each with special Christmas gifts that year, consisting of healing and forgiveness, compassion, love, and understanding. For me, I believe it was the grace and mercy of God that Daddy and I were able to give forgiveness and receive forgiveness, then healing grew from there.

When I shared this story with someone close to me, her response was, "I'm glad you and your dad made peace before he died because you try talking to a tombstone."

To this day, those words have haunted me. She had terrible, unresolved problems with her father, and tragically, he died suddenly, leaving nothing resolved; it was too late. I felt very sad for her, as she never had or now would ever have the opportunity to express her feelings to him or work out their differences. To this day, I believe she carries much guilt around because of all those unresolved differences.

We often wonder why we ourselves or someone else has to go through such immense and inconceivable suffering and why God, at times, seems to not be present or why He's so silent. I do not presume to have any kind of answers to these thoughts or questions. Maybe my dad was meant to endure all that he did so God could heal a part of him that had been broken all his life and, in the process, also provide healing grace while teaching my family and me some valuable lessons. God can bring beauty and meaning out of the worst circumstances, even suffering. We can't possibly ever see God's master plan, but I believe everything happens for a reason and God's timing is perfect.

The greatest gift tragedy can bring and teach is that it forces us to reconsider the things in life we may have been taking for granted. I've learned this even through my own loss and grief, as I suffer daily with my own debilitating condition. Tragedy has changed my perspective of what is truly important in life and what real gifts are. No material Christmas gifts, fancy holiday parties, or high Christmas fashion could have ever compared to what our Lord Jesus had taught and given to me that especially tough Christmas year. Lessons in forgiveness, healing, grace, compassion, love, and understanding are what really matter. These are gifts that truly last and are free from our Lord Jesus above. All we need to do is repent of our sins, ask, and be willing to receive with open hearts and minds the unconditional love of Christ to come and live within us. Our relationships with others and with God, our creator, are everlasting and fade-resistant. No amount of wealth or material possessions can buy true happiness or heal failing health. Only God heals, and sometimes, it comes about in the most unexpected ways, even to someone who is physically dying. When my dad died that Christmas, he didn't have a penny to his name and very few possessions to call his own. Yet when he died, he died knowing he could and had chosen to freely give and also to freely receive forgiveness, healing, and God's grace, and that made him and me both rich in heavenly treasure—in which no amount of money could ever buy.

The true meaning of Christmas for me is to celebrate our Savior's birth. Jesus came into this world to renew everything and to redeem mankind in the eyes of God. He brings love, hope, peace, compassion, forgiveness, and healing. Jesus makes a way for each of us to be with Him in heaven one day, as He sacrificed His life on the cross so that we may live and have everlasting life and eternal peace with Him forever.

Every Christmas, I think of my daddy and what he's doing in heaven for Christmas. I believe and it is my constant hope and prayer that God's mercy totally now has healed him in body, mind, and spirit. Instead of becoming angry at God for taking my dad at the most special time of the year, my heart swelled with gratitude for our Lord Jesus for opening my heart and soul, allowing grace, compassion, and mercy to fill me so that I could forgive and also to apologize and accept Daddy's forgiveness. By making a choice to do this, our gracious heavenly Father gave me and Dad a meaningful relationship before it was forever too late. I was so grateful to God for the healing that had taken place just in two short years, getting to know Daddy in a way I had never known him before, having many deep conversations, reflecting back and being able to be civilized about it. Listening to his terrible life story, the horrible depression which had plagued him for years, the extreme sadness and regret he had for everything he had ever caused, and the chronic physical illness of which he was now dying brought many tears to my eyes. He had lost everything he had, including his family. He truly was a broken man in every aspect of his life. My heart, which for so many years had held so much bitterness, anger, and resentment, was truly changed because of God's understanding, which He gave to me, as well as through His mercy and grace.

We serve an awesome God, and He forgives each one of us, and in turn, our Lord gave me the grace to forgive and tell my dad I loved him—those three words that growing up I never could have truly said with any meaning because of all the pain, fear, and damage he had caused, which, now, I had truly forgiven him of. God comforted me after my daddy's death, reminding me he had died knowing that I loved him and forgave him. I also knew he loved me and had received my forgiveness, and I had accepted his. For me, that Christmas is what I considered a true gift from our Lord in heaven above. I had always believed in my heart that if someday I could truly forgive my dad, then I knew God already had—that was always my prayer and hope. To this day, I still have much thanks and gratitude to my Lord Jesus for bringing such beauty and meaning to me out of a lifetime of suffering for both me and my dad.

That painful year at Christmas, God taught me about the importance of healing broken relationships, showing true compassion and mercy for others who consistently wrong us, giving and receiving forgiveness, which I never thought possible because of the horrible mess and severe dysfunction in my family. Most importantly, God revealed to me how valuable showing others kindness, understanding, and love is, even in the worst circumstances of a person's life, those suffering with unrelenting sickness and disease, emotional pain, physical pain, and all types of adversities along the way. Through my two-year reconciliation with Daddy, watching his helpless suffering and his untimely death, God brought about this understanding to me, and as stated previously, I continue to be grateful for the irreplaceable healing times with him before he died. I am so thankful to our Lord and Savior for coming into my heart—allowing His light of mercy and forgiving grace to shine through me, enabling me to appreciate and to recognize the precious gifts and lessons He bestowed upon me, my daddy, and our entire family that most difficult season in my life, once upon a Christmastime.

*The fruit of the Spirit is love, joy, peace, patience, kindness,
goodness, faithfulness, gentleness and self-control.
Against such things there is no law.*
—Galatians 5:22–23

*Be kind to one another, tenderhearted, forgiving
one another, as God in Christ forgave you.*
—Ephesians 4:32

For nothing will be impossible with God.
—Luke 1:37

Soul Searching

A Prayer of Regret and Reflection

What do I say to all the years gone by, of the memories that always make me cry?

What do I do with the feelings I feel? Should I hide them away or pour out my heart, for what can anyone now do or even say?

How should I feel when you are lying there dying and I'm the only one standing alone, left crying?

How do I answer why you have no friends, when, now, they've all left and are gone like the wind?

How do I be your friend, when you never reached out to take my hand?

How should I forgive for what you've done, when thoughts of the pain erase memories of the fun?

What happened to the beautiful days, where we both felt God's presence and shared the warmth of the summer sun?

How do I say I'm sorry for the things that I've said, when all I can see is you lying unresponsive in that hospital bed?

How can I possibly make you understand what our family's
been through, when nobody cared or could ever take the time to say,
"I love you"?

> *Even though I walk through the valley of the*
> *shadow of death, I will fear no evil.*
> *For you are with me; your rod and your staff, they comfort me.*
> —Psalm 23:4

Golden Staircase to Heaven

*A Prayer of Intense Suffering, Faith in God's
Comfort, and the Hope of Heaven*

In this quiet place from where I sit and write,
I cry from the daily tortuous and exhausting physical pain—
from a rare disease
that no one can feel and that no one sees.
I begin to pray, hoping You, Jesus, will hear me,
as I tearfully mourn the person I used to be.
Please, Jesus, hear my prayer,
for it is my constant faith through tireless adversity
that allows me to believe You really care and are truly there for
me.
All alone in the stillness of the night, I look for You, Jesus,
my Messiah, the one who makes all things new for everyone,
who believes in
and prays to You.

Do you not see the tears that fall from my tired, swollen eyes
or feel the sadness from the tormenting physical pain that fills my
weakened soul?
I wish I could find my way to be with You, Jesus, in heaven,
leaving this painful earthly world behind, for it has nothing
that I truly desire, only disease, sickness, and pain that afflicts all of
mankind.

Suffering so in my human shell, when I cannot get well,
why must I continue to be here?
For it has always been with You, Lord, that I wish to dwell.
My purpose anymore I cannot find,
through pain, tears, and chronic disability,
yet You, Lord, continue to give me strength to keep me humble
and kind.

I will always continue to pray, to call upon your holy name, as
I once again ask:
"Please, Jesus, bring me comfort from all sickness and ongoing
debilitating pain."
I watch as the spring rain begins to fall, wishing it could wash
away my sorrows and suffering so I would not have to keep enduring
this all.
The intense physical pain makes me feel like a caged animal
with no way out;
thus, keeping me in a psychological prison where my emotions
are always so raw.
Jesus, you have given me many blessings in this life,
while forgiving me my many sins in Your loving sight.
Your mercy is endless, Your love so great; why must I go on in
this painful condition and for heaven must I continue to wait?
There is an undeniable yearning inside of me, O Lord,
wanting to come home to You to be made anew.
I pray for healing in my painful body, as well as for comfort
and peace for my crushed and broken spirit that only You, Lord, can
understand, knowing the degree of pain my body continues to suffer
through.
Please, Lord, take my hand and say, "Come home," and I will
surely follow.

I dream of a golden path in the middle of a tranquil sea with
Your angels leading—and escorting me to a marvelous staircase,

beautifully embellished with the most vivid and wonderfully fragrant flowers.

A majestic hidden staircase right here in the middle of this starlit sea

that sparkles, shimmers, and waits for me.

I gaze up at this miraculously wonderful sight, where I see You, Jesus, standing at the top, the entrance into heaven.

With arms open wide and Your unconditional love smiling down, You gently call my name, ready to embrace me, holding me close by Your side.

Here in this calming place, the reflection of the twilit water on heaven's luminous stairs

casts a beautiful, soft golden glow that radiates from high above the heavens to earth far down here below.

I once again behold Your heavenly divine angels, aligning heaven's majestic staircase,

as high as the human eye can see.

The beautiful angels of light are gazing down, smiling upon me.

Instantly, I feel such immense peace, comfort, and serenity, as I eagerly long to take that first golden step upward, to my heavenly destiny.

Traveling this magnificent hidden staircase to heaven with angels leading

is truly the most precious gift I could have ever hoped to receive.

Away from this broken world, away from my earthly painful human vessel,

where only my longing soul resides, my broken spirit wants to soar free to You, Jesus,

where You will welcome me with unconditional loving arms outstretched wide.

There, I will be in Your ever-loving presence, forever by Your side.

This beautiful journey, ascending higher and higher, I desperately must climb.

With thoughts only of reaching You, my Lord and Savior, on my mind,
transcending every earthly obstacle, crossing all barriers of time.

The golden staircase to heaven, I wish to climb,
here on this ever so calming sea, where the angels of Jesus have led me.

Their comforting presence enveloping all around, as they soar by my side.

Escorting me with their peaceful faces from this world of painful suffering,
I want to escape and hide.

Seeking refuge in my Lord and Savior Jesus, who for me was crucified then
died.

He gave His life in unconditional love, so I could live mine—
to enjoy the beauty on this earth for one yet brief moment in time.

Now, in the middle of this amazing moonlit sea,
the beauty of heaven's illuminating staircase is shown
and offered freely from Jesus to me.

Adorned with beautiful flowers, bursting with the most magnificent colors,
the soft picturesque golden glow of the staircase winds around into the highest heavens.

I marvel at its majesty and untouched radiant beauty, as I step to begin my climb.

Ahead of me, the golden stairs to heaven are velvety soft,
as if stepping onto a fluffy cloud made out of the finest gold silken cloth.

Fragrances so sweet and pure fill my senses, as my eyes continue to behold the breathtaking, remarkable beauty of heaven's hidden staircase that the Lord
is showing me.
As I climb higher, the colors in the sky become brighter and more vividly exquisite.
Pinks, yellows, oranges, purples, and reds, an abundance of colors,
as if all were melting together on a painter's palette, opening up the beauty of heaven,
just as I had dreamed it would be.

In the far-off distance, I hear heavenly music—all different types,
in perfect symphonious harmony.
As I continue my steps toward heaven on this beautifully hidden staircase
in the middle of God's moonlit sea,
sweet heavenly melodies of song calm and begin to soothe me.
My mind is filled with only peaceful thoughts of spending my life with Thee—
with You, Jesus, in heaven's paradise of eternity.
As I begin to grow tired from much pain, peaceful angels are now carrying me.
Almost there, I wearily gaze up and see the sweet face of Jesus, standing, smiling,
arms reaching out to me in unconditional love, welcoming me home into heaven's
peaceful serenity.

The golden staircase to heaven is for all to climb,
here on this ever so calming and peaceful sea,
where the angels of Jesus have led both you and me.
Their comforting presence enveloping all around, as they soar by all

who desire them by their side.

The angels escort all humanity with their peaceful faces from this world

of painful suffering into God's perfect heavenly realm.

Seeking refuge in our Lord and Savior, Jesus,

who for all of humankind was crucified then died.

He gave His life in unconditional love so all His children could live

to enjoy the beauty of this earth for one yet brief moment in time.

Now, in the middle of this amazing moonlit sea,

the beauty of heaven's illuminating staircase is shown

and offered freely from Jesus to all who come to Him,

believing and wanting to receive.

The golden staircase of heaven is for everyone,

as Jesus invites ALL to come—to be in perfect relationship with Him.

At the top of the majestic staircase, He will be waiting, smiling with open arms

to welcome each and every weary one of us to enter into heaven's glorious paradise, where we will spend blissful eternity and be one with Him.

> *The Kingdom of Heaven is like a treasure hidden in*
> *the field, which a man found and hid again;*
> *and from joy over it he goes and sells all that he has and buys that field.*
> *Again, the Kingdom of Heaven is like a merchant seeking fine pearls,*
> *and upon finding one pearl of great value, he went*
> *and sold all that he had and bought it.*
> —Matthew 13:44–46

*But God, rich in mercy, because of the great
love with which He loved us,
even when we were dead in our trespasses,
made us alive together with Christ—
by grace you have been saved.*
—Ephesians 2:4–5

My Prayer

A Conversation with Jesus about
Suffering, Faith, and Hope

Please, Jesus, I humbly ask that You hear my prayer.

I pray that You walk with me through this ever so dark valley in my life.

Please clasp my hand tightly, never letting go, for I want to believe You love me so.

Promise You will never leave or forsake me.

Even in faith, I continue to stumble, fall, and have myself questioned believing,

while living and struggling in my worst pain states.

Please, Lord, forgive me as I cry

because the constant pain strips my life away,

and all I can do is continue to pray.

I seek You in all I do, for my hope is in heaven, where I will one day see You.

Dear Jesus, I desperately need You,

as my prayers are for strength, wisdom, and endurance.

Please grant me the will to continue to live and to serve others,

just as You have taught to me to do.

How do I accomplish this with such physical limitations

and such terrible, debilitating chronic pain?

My body and soul wrestle constantly with this, for it is true
divine healing from You
that I seek and continually wish.

I listen for your voice directing me what to do
but am so weary; all I want to do is go to heaven and be with
You.
My fears are strong and this terrible physical disability so real.
Please, Jesus, place your comforting hand on me, telling me to
"be still."
Help me to hear when You speak,
for often I cannot because the pain is strong and I am so terribly
weak.
Jesus, if You're really there, then please listen and respond to my
prayer.

See and feel the sadness, as I continue to weep,
for my prayers to You I will continue to keep.
You are my Lord and Savior; please never leave my side,
granting me strength through all the pain to always abide.
I feel so lost, cut off from the world, suffering in my body so,
that my tired and weakened spirit just wants to go.
Longing to separate from my body prison of pain,
I pray for Your angels to carry my soul swiftly to You, Jesus,
on a feather of an angel's wing.

In heaven, out of my mouth, praises to You I will repeatedly
sing.
I continue to call and cry out in my hour of need,
O Lord, respond favorably to me please.
Hear me, O Lord, for I cannot possibly bear this life anymore;
I just want You to rescue me through heaven's narrow door.
Please, Jesus, do not abandon Your hurting child,
but instead, scoop me up into Your loving arms, even for just a
little while.

Please help me, for I cannot possibly go on like this with the amount of physical pain

I try and hide, as I continue to suffer daily with no relief.

Dear Jesus, please strengthen my faith and rip out the weeds of unbelief.

All alone and sad, once a vibrant life, now lost,

tears continuing to glisten down my cheeks.

Please, Jesus, send Your guardian angels this night

to come gather me up and usher me into Your loving sight,

as I do not want to continue this earthly fight.

Hear my prayer, O Lord, when I call to You

to please remove this great affliction, as I continue to cry again and again.

I pray You will come near my side

to embrace Your hurting child with unconditional love, with arms open wide.

I do not know what to do anymore, as I physically cannot continue

to bear this amount of suffering with absolutely no way out.

Lord, I humbly ask for forgiveness, as my weakened soul starts to doubt.

The physical pain not only weakens my body but also my mind.

I search earnestly for You in prayer because it is You that I wish to find.

Please bring me peace like I've never known before

and come into my heart, I humbly pray,

never ever to leave me, for to You and the Holy Spirit I do continually pray.

Jesus, You are the way, the truth, and the life (John 14:6).

I so desire to walk with You forever in Your loving sight.

Please take my hand and lead me out of the darkness and into the light,

never to let go, no matter how difficult the road is which lies ahead.

Please continue to hold my hand, even when the journey becomes so difficult
that only pure tears of pain, I am only able to shed.
Jesus, please do not cast me away, as I struggle to live every day
with insurmountable pain, anguish, anger, and severe disability.

Please remove this anger from me, for it serves no purpose in my life
and is not an emotion I want to carry with me.
Rip it away and replace it with soothing peace, abundant joy, and everlasting love
that only You can send to me from heaven above.
I have prayed to You to come be the Lord and Savior of my life,
to calm Your weeping child facing such overwhelming strife
and so much uncertainty in this life.
Thank You, Lord, for giving me the words, thoughts,
and prayers to which I sit and continue to write.

I am in the darkest valley in my life, not knowing
how to move forward or how to stop the agonizing pain.
Please, Jesus, once again, I humbly pray for You to take my hand,
staying with me Lord, never letting me go, even when I constantly disappoint
You with my thoughts and actions, as I cry in shame;
please forgive me and forever light my way with Your ever-loving kindness
and Your unconditional forgiveness, never casting any blame.
I come to You honestly from a great place of pain
that most people could never understand or ever even explain.

My relationship with You, Jesus, I desire to be genuine and real.
I wish to express sincere prayers for others, as well as giving to You my thanksgiving,

praise, tears, deepest thoughts, and fears, as You are aware of my ongoing frustrations,
as well as a continued deep desire to be healed.
Jesus, please take over my life in every way;
I give You control over my painfully weakened physical body and broken soul,
hoping for divine healing in Your time; I continue to pray.
If healing does not come, please take me to heaven
So I do not continue to suffer on this earth one more day.

Please use me in whatever way to serve Your purpose, for Your will be done;
I truly believe and confess You are the Messiah and God's only begotten Son.
I know Your ways are higher than mine, but I truly do not understand the suffering
I must continue to bear and find my searching mind wandering—
are You, Jesus, really there and, to Your hurting child, do You even care?

What wonderful plan do You have for my life, when all I see,
feel, and experience is physical pain, depression, loneliness,
and the loss of my life as I once knew?
Please, Jesus, hear my crying prayer to You,
taking my hand and holding me forever close.
Help me to feel your unconditional loving presence that You are truly there for me,
when beyond the pain and tears, I just cannot see;
please, Jesus, I humbly pray You will never ever abandon me. Amen.

For as the heavens are higher than the earth,
so are My ways higher than your ways and
My thoughts than your thoughts.

—Isaiah 55:9

I love those who love Me, and those who seek Me diligently find Me.
—Proverbs 8:17

Never will I leave you: never will I forsake you.
—Hebrews 13:5

My Furry Blessing

A Prayer of Thanksgiving for My Companion Animal

The journey of this earthly life is full of twist and turns,
resulting in many valuable lessons we can each learn.
All suffering is difficult to accept, whether one can see outward
physical pain and disability or from an invisible illness—
appearing fine to others but silently coping with a disease and
pain that no one can see or even understand.
It is only natural, when we are in pain, to call out to God, wanting it to end.
We ask Him how long we must endure, if it will stop, and when.

The Lord walks beside us through every step of our lives.
We can't see Him or even, at times, feel His presence;
only by our faith do we acknowledge that He is really there.
By opening our hearts and minds, we can see His love and comfort in many different ways.
God reveals Himself to us through the kindness of a stranger,
help from a family member or friend,
through the beauty of nature, or in a beautiful melody that
touches our soul.
A painter who paints a beautiful, serene scene, God breathes
beauty and meaning into their artwork through every careful
brushstroke.

To each and every one of us, He gives us a gift of peace and also of hope.

One of the many ways God may comfort us is through the unconditional love of an animal. Alone for most of my day, the Lord has blessed me with a small, white schnauzer as my companion and friend.

I have affectionately nicknamed her my precious little puppy girl.

She brings me much joy and peace in times of loneliness and sorrow.

I thank God for her, as she comforts me when I'm crying and in pain.

A lick, a playful tail wag, or the tilt of her head while looking at me brings a smile to my tearful face.

Placing her small, white paws in my lap, she crawls up upon me with comforting eyes and attentive ears.

She sees my heart breaking with isolation and suffering, often with painful tears.

God has given me this amazing bond with her, despite my illness being debilitating and having no cure.

I remember when I was growing up, how the softness of a bunny or the peaceful gaze of my pony captured my heart.

A soft meow from a kitten or the crying of a small puppy awakened much empathy within me.

Colorful birds, a baby lamb, or a newborn calf learning to take its first steps all developed my love and appreciation for animals.

They spoke to my heart and soul, as my spirit was deeply touched by their innocence.

The Lord was allowing me to share in this beautiful world with the creatures He had created.

These were His precious animals for which He had given me so much gratitude, compassion, and love.

Thank You, God, for my sweet little puppy girl.

She lies and sleeps beside me, as I sit and write through all hours of the night.

I gaze at her sleeping peacefully, watching her breathe softly, as I stroke her soft white fur; she neither moves nor stirs.

Her slumbering body is nestled up against mine;
her little soul is as comforting as it is kind.

She is aware of my emotions, whether happy, sad, or suffering with unrelenting pain.

Animals may not be able to speak, but I believe there is a shared unspoken language between a person and their companion animal.

Just as she comforts me in many ways when I'm ill and in pain,
I comfort her with unconditional love just the same.

When she's sick or sad, I hold her near, like a mother comforts her child.

She puts her small head on my shoulder, as I talk quietly to her about how much she is loved by me and by God.

Stroking her white soft fur, I never want to let her go because I love and cherish her so.

This bond that we have was appointed by God above and given to us both to share.

I continually thank God for my comforting companion, my sweet little puppy girl.

God gave her to me years ago to cherish and to love; I took care of her as I watched her mature and grow;

Her innocence and unconditional love are treasured gifts the Lord has blessed me with from heaven above.

She is getting older now, so time is even more precious with my special gift from God.

I remember that joyous day many years ago, when she was placed into my arms as a tiny, beautiful puppy.

I will be there the day she draws her last breath, closes her eyes, and slumbers softly back into the loving arms of God.

Tearfully, I will kiss her goodbye.

I will give thanks to the Lord for all the wonderful years He gave me with my loving companion, Pay-Lay.

To me, she will always have a special place in my heart and will forever be my sweet baby—my precious little puppy girl.

> *Though all creatures are subject to man's*
> *cruelty, God loves all His creation*
> *and has made plans for His children and the lesser*
> *creatures to enjoy His eternal kingdom.*
> —Psalm 145:9–10, 13, 15–21 AMP

Goodbye to My Furry Blessing

*A Prayer of Grief and Loss for My
Beloved Companion Animal*

As I sob, my heart is breaking in two;
I just can't say goodbye to you.
You look at me with your dark, sad eyes—
it is as if you know that I can't bear to let you go.
I pick you up to hold and love you, and your body is weak and
limp.

I remember the day, just short weeks ago,
when the veterinarian told us that, soon, you would go.
I was in such a state of shock and disbelief,
trying to cope with my overwhelming grief.

Hearing what was said about you not having long,
I prayed and cried, "Lord, let the doctors be wrong!"
But the images were clear, the cancer was there;
it was time for a plan, not time for despair.

We opted for Pawspice, that's hospice for pets—
comfort care only, guided by the vets,
meds to ease symptoms and a checklist to follow;
Eat what you want while you can still swallow.

The Lord blessed me with you for so many years;
now, watching you die, I am grief-stricken and in tears.
I'm losing you, and I feel so helpless.
I'm watching you slip away before my eyes.
You've been my constant companion, ever by my side.

Such a comfort you've been in my sickness and pain;
I pray, "Lord, please allow her to remain.
I can't bear letting her go because I love her so."

My heart is heavy, as I search for strength and peace.
I tell you to fight the cancer, but I see how tired you are.
At times, you can't even raise your head in your bed, as your
breathing is labored.

I believe the Lord is near you, as you prepare for your end;
despite my sorrow, I must let you go, my furry friend.

Thank you, my little puppy girl, for all the years of love and
care;
no one will ever understand the bond that we share.
I could never watch you suffer with this life-robbing disease;
I see you lying there dying, trying to breathe.

Perhaps you remember when the day came
That you couldn't move when I said your name.
I knew it was time then I had to be strong;
God gave me strength, and it didn't take long.

I hope that a heaven was waiting for you,
where illness has vanished and you're better than new.
I hope that you're playing and haven't a care,
and I hope that you'll think of me while you are there.

I look up through tearstained eyes to ask the Lord why?
Why does she have to go *now*?
Lord, why a few more years with me will You not allow?

> *In His hand is the life of every living thing*
> *and the breath of all mankind.*
>
> —Job 12:10

> *Your righteousness is like the highest mountains, your justice like*
> *the great deep. You, Lord, preserve both people and animals.*
>
> —Psalm 36:6

Blessed Savior, Please See and Comfort Me

A Prayer of Deep Suffering, Thanksgiving, Peace, and Serenity

Blessed Savior, You are here with me in my hours of constant suffering, as You guide and lovingly comfort me.

Through my beautiful memories of Your majestic sea,

You convey the warmth of Your love and Your surrounding presence to me.

My frail body and weary eyes behold the magnificent storms on the sea,

a reminder, an unwanted thorn of the relentless pain that ever torments me.

You, Lord, reveal the beautiful, peaceful serenity of the sea—the way I remember it to be.

As the waves calm, so You soothe and bring comfort to my soul.

I remember the beauty of the sun shining over the blue sea;

I basked in its warming rays, reveled, and smiled as the cool whitecaps splashed upon me.

The smell of salty air brings back vivid memories of the days when I was once so close to You, Lord, and to the sea.

I would walk along the shore, gazing out at a watery desert,

as the waves would gently wash over me.

In awe at its magnificence, I watched the crashing waves and could see
and feel You, Lord, in the beauty and power of the sea.

While on the shore, I would gaze at the water and wonder if You could hear me when I prayed to You.
In my heart, I had always hoped You knew my name and could *see* me too, Your little girl who loved and called out to You.
Looking below the surface of the water, I saw the beauty and quietness of the world beneath, as if it was reaching up to me,
God's creatures gliding about so peaceful and free.
Seeing the tropical fish brings a palette of radiance, like the colors of the rainbow,
shining from below.

Blessed Savior, You lull the waves softly to sleep,
bringing me to a place of great quietness and peace.
Your steadfastness is unending.
You, Lord, are the only one who sees how the everyday pain brings me to tears.
My life is like a fragile glass ball, enduring many cracks, only to fall apart and break.
Please come and relieve me of my sorrow and suffering as my life,
Lord, is only Yours to take.
Blessed Savior, I seek Your holy face, while humbly bowing down before You with gratitude and grace.
I want nothing of this world, as I am tormented in a painful decaying shell,
waking up daily to my own personal hell.
My dream and desire is to be escorted into heaven, for only there
Will I find peace and comfort with You, my blessed Savior.

You've shown me Your glory and majesty in my wonderful memories of the sea,
a place where I came to know and communicate with Thee.

Lord, I pray for Your continued presence and mercy upon me.
Please draw near, when I cry my own sea of tears.
Tenderly hold me so I may feel Your unconditional love and healing, as it encircles me.
Thank You, Lord, for coming to me in my brokenness and pain,
in my beautiful memories and dreams of Your majestic sea—
where I find joy and happiness with You amid the sorrow and pain.
Blessed Savior, I pray, please do not forsake
But always love and forever *sea* and comfort me. Amen

*The Lord is near to the brokenhearted and
saves those who are crushed in spirit.*
—Psalm 34:18

Where Are You?

A Prayer of Deep Suffering, Isolation, and Loneliness

In my abyss of loneliness and pain, I'm sinking yet further down.
Where are You, my Lord?
I have called out to You but have been left in silence.
These painful disease processes are robbing me of a meaningful life,
and my endurance is growing dim.

I ask myself, "Which is worse, the medicines with their many side effects or the diseases themselves?"
Looking in the mirror, I realize I do not recognize the reflection staring back.
All the medicines used to combat the disease have completely changed my appearance.
"Who are you?" I cry and say to myself, "This can't be me," and yet sadly, it is.
I have lost the person I used to be.

Trapped within this body that doesn't work anymore, my mind altered by unrelenting pain and the meds used to fight it,
I'm trying to cope with what seems an impossible situation.
This is not the way I wanted or expected my life to be.
I do not want to fight anymore.

     PATRICIA ANNE "PATTI" MEITZLER DAVIS

I want to lay my burdens down at the feet of my God.

My soul yearns for You, O Lord, to heal my broken body and to set me free.

I do not want to go on—I long for Your embrace, but it does not come.

Why have You forsaken me, when illness and pain are piling on top of me?

I'm drowning and seeking comfort and protection under Your mighty wing of love.

My world is filled with despair, not one friend who could ever understand or take the time to care.

I dream, and my soul longs for heaven—to be in Your loving arms, my Lord,

where all my tears will be wiped away and sickness and disease will have had their day.

My body aches, and my soul longs to come home to You, O my Lord.

Do You not see the frailness and brokenness of my worn body?

My suffering soul only longs for You, Lord, as it has my whole life.

In my fear and pain, I question, "Is heaven really real?"

I believe this to be true, but my faith is shaken.

I have been forgotten by many people, but You, Lord—where are You?

For I cannot feel Your presence.

Perhaps it is the pain and medications that cloud my thoughts and judgment.

Are You beside me, crying with me? Hurting when I hurt?

Holding me up, when I continue to fall?

I feel as though I'm waiting to die; the highlights of my life have all passed by.

So much loss I've had to endure, and now, my life hangs in a
fragile balance,
drifting from one day to the next, afraid what will happen if the
pain becomes too intense.
I need You, Lord.

Where are You when I sit up nights crying in unrelenting pain?
Tears falling on the pages, as I struggle to continue writing my
thoughts, prayers, and deepest desires to You, my Lord.
Once a calm and gentle spirit I was; now, I am in a state of unrest.
Please come to me, my Lord, and rescue me, as I have no joy
or peace.

Where are You, my Lord? Come, take my life please,
for I want this pain and disability to cease.
In the midst of extreme loneliness and in the isolation of ongo-
ing pain, I realize just how cruel and unfair life can be.
It goes on, no matter how disabled I become.
In the circle of life, we are born, we live, then we die.
This suffering makes me hate my life.
I go to bed, and I'm trapped in my prison of pain.
I wake up, and it starts all over again.
I am not living, just struggling and trying to survive.
Please, Lord, show Your face unto me.

I do not want to live in this fallen world anymore.
I want to die, to say goodbye to everything I once loved.
It means nothing to me anymore, as the pain envelopes my
body and has destroyed the person I once was.
Calling out to You, O Lord, but no answer do I receive.
Why have You hidden Your face from me?

I do not know what to do or even how to talk to You.
People do not realize what those others suffering intensely go
through.

Many days, it is about living moment by moment,
and when each moment is filled with grueling pain,
it changes a person, and they are never the same.
Many say life is a gift, but intense suffering may make one question this.
I personally do not want a long life anymore;
fighting intense pain every day has drained me to the core.

My weary soul so often cries out and hungers for You, O Lord.
Please make Yourself known to me, Lord,
For I am wandering in the darkness of this suffering, even though my eyes see the light of day.

A good friend reminds me, "Pain and grief make children of all of us."
I find this statement is so true for me.
I cry like a child when the pain is too much to bear.
Just as children cry when they are in pain and need the comfort of their parent,
I, too, cry often and want You, Lord, my Father in heaven
to embrace me as Your daughter and take this painful disease from me.
I cannot focus on anything else, at times, because the pain is all-encompassing.
Not many people understand this type of physical pain, but it is real, and it exists.
I try to write what it is like living in my body, calling out to You,
My Lord and Savior, for mercy.
I pray for others, who I do not know, who are suffering
with unrelenting diseases and pain.

I truly believe in You, Lord, for all good and wondrous things.
If I could see You as Your disciples did, I would crawl on my hands and knees;
with my very last breath, I would come to You, Lord.

For You are holy and good and the God of eternal love.

I see You in the purity of a white-winged dove.

My eyes follow the white dove, able to soar over mountains and oceans.

It lives and does not know imprisonment of any kind, only freedom.

Like the beautiful white dove, I long to be free

and to move without pain and disability.

Please come and heal me so I may once again fly and soar in my own life

and that it may be pleasing unto You.

Oh, my precious Lord, do You not hear or see me in the dark abyss of my pain?

Like the white-winged dove, I am very fragile and in need of Your loving and healing care.

O Lord, please do not cast me away, as my heart and soul thirst for You and for Your righteousness.

Nothing in this life can bring me the peace and comfort I so desperately seek, except for You, my Lord.

No one hears my cries and no one sees.

Oh, my precious Lord, why have You forsaken me?

Search my soul and see—for You it cries.

So close to You, I wish to be.

Please, my Lord, my Lord, never forsake or abandon me. Amen.

Out of the depths have I cried unto you, O Lord.
—Psalm 130:1 KJV

Reflections—Going Home

Dear Father in heaven,

As my time draws to a close here on earth and I prepare for my heavenly home with You, I wanted to write this letter. I have many questions for You that were never answered during my lifetime. Even though I did not receive those answers, maybe after I'm gone, others who suffer—and who may read this letter—may identify with some of these difficult questions. It is my hope that this letter may help someone else who is struggling and suffering.

Why was I born? What is my purpose? Is this life a test or a trial run for our true home with You in heaven? Your Word teaches us that we are all born for a purpose and that Your purpose is the greatest in saving all of Your children.

When we are born, everyone wants to come and see the new little one, God's own miracle. As we grow, our thoughts, emotions, and perceptions of the world are shaped by many experiences, including interactions with others, both good and bad. Usually, as children, we have many around us to love and support us, but this is not always the case. We are taught that life is a gift from You, Father. Society sets forth rules and expectations for how one is supposed to conduct oneself. If we have an outgoing nature, we may have many friends.

Before my illness, I was blessed to have a wonderful group of friends. I had an outgoing personality and loved life. I remember having conversations with some of those friends about how we would *always* be there for each other, no matter what difficulties we faced in our lives. But nothing lasts forever, and when I became ill, those promises were broken.

My dear Father, this is what has hurt me the worst. When my friends stopped calling and coming around, it hurt me to the very core. One friend said to me, "If you are going to cry, I have to hang up the phone—I just can't take it." Another person said, "You can talk to me about anything you want, just not about your pain."

I have come to realize that these people, too, are Your children, and we all fall short of glory. Statements like this come from ignorance; some people genuinely do not know what to say to someone who is ill. I now understand this, Father, as you have brought other people into my life, who are also suffering greatly. Their stories are familiar to me—the misunderstandings, unfair judgments, loss of friends—and I can see how those broken relationships add to their distress.

Father, I am grateful to You for my fond memories of those people who are now gone from me. You have provided me with many blessings in my life. Thank You for the opportunities for growth that You have placed before me. I believe I have a stronger, closer relationship with You through my pain and illness, as I have chosen to turn to You rather than away.

To those friends whom I was once so angry with, those who have left my life and judged me, I want you to know that I have forgiven you. It was a process, but with my Father's help, I have prayed for you to be blessed. Thank You for your presence in my life, even if it was only for a season. I learned things from each and every one of you. I realize now that forgiveness does not always mean reconciliation, and I am okay with that. I thank my Father in heaven for the blessing of forgiveness.

Now, I am very weary, and it is time to lay down my pen and say a final prayer. I will close my eyes and rest. Thank You, Father, for my life and for all the people who came into my world. I love you, Father, and I am ready now to come home and have You embrace me as a daughter in Your beautiful kingdom of eternal life—heaven.

> *For I reckon that the sufferings of this present*
> *time are not worthy to be compared*
> *with the glory which shall be revealed in us.*
> —Romans 8:17–18 KJV

A Dream, My Day with Jesus, Abba (Dearest) Father

A Prayer of Suffering, Healing, Joy, and Hope in Our Lord and Savior, Jesus Christ

I seek You, Lord, with all of my heart;
from this earthly world, my painful body wishes to depart.
Into Your loving arms, I give myself to You.
No matter how much I may suffer in this world, Jesus,
You will always be my Savior and Lord.
I long to be in Your loving presence and to have You by my side forevermore.

In my broken body filled with pain, my weary soul calls out to You.
Every day, I dream of heaven, of being with You, Abba Father (dearest Father).
I look beyond this life on earth and long to be in a beautiful and peaceful place.
My whole being aches to finally rest in Your safe, loving arms and to behold Your most holy face.

I lay my head on my pillow, hoping to be comfortable while trying to get away from my pain—eventually, I drift into a sweet, deep sleep.

Angels carry me off in my dream and take me to the most beautiful place that I have ever seen.

I start to walk on this serene and captivating beach,
where the sky is blue and the winds are soft and gentle, brushing across my face.
I feel joy, like I have never felt before, and a calming peace sweeps across me, a knowing that all will be well.
The cool, pure water flows over my feet, as they sink into the warm sand.
I hear the thunderous waves crashing in the distance.
The sun bathes me in love, light, and warmth.
No pain in my body do I now feel,
for I know that in this beautiful place, it has all been healed.

I turn around and see my precious Lord Jesus smiling.
He is walking toward me, calling my name.
An overwhelming love emanates from His holy face.
In His arms, He is carrying my beloved puppy girl, Pele.
She is alive and healed from the terrible cancer.
She is snow-white and more beautiful than ever before.
She recognizes me and begins to bark with delight,
then runs to me once Jesus carefully puts her paws on the sand.

It is such a joyous reunion to have her back in my arms once again.
She licks my face, tail wagging, as I shed tears of happiness and gratitude.
I begin to laugh and hold Pele close, as I spin around joyfully,
telling her how much I missed and cried over her when she died.
When I put Pele down, she runs to Jesus, and He takes her in His arms and says to me,
"Behold, I make all things new" (Revelation 21:5).

I say, "Amen," and acknowledge that Jesus has miraculously healed me too.

Jesus, Pele, and I begin to walk together along the shore on this perfect sunny day.

I look out to see the whitecaps frothing at our feet;
the tide ebbs and flows in a rhythmic dance.
I start to run, hop, and skip, like I did when I was a child
before this painful disease destroyed my body.
The constant pain I suffered with every day is gone.
As long as I am with my Lord Jesus, no harm or sickness will befall me or my precious Pele again.

I am so elated by spirit soars over the turquoise sea, singing praises to the Lord of lords.

This is the most beautiful place that I have ever been to, I tell Jesus.

I see mountains with white waterfalls cascading down.
As the waves continue to roll upon the sands, Pele plays and frolics with no fear.

I am so overjoyed to see her alive, happy, and well.
I thank Jesus for her healing, as well as for mine.

Jesus asks me if I want to do something fun, and I say, "Yes."
He says, "Come, follow me."
Jesus starts to walk on the water, and I follow with Pele by my side.

Jesus says, "Have no fear but have faith."
I am now walking on the water, following Jesus onto the sea with my dear Pele beside me.

Jesus takes my hand and smiles at me and says, "Keep following me."

I begin to fear as the sea grows stormy, but Jesus calms the waves, and the winds grow still.

Then He stops and says, "Look down."

I see the most beautiful creatures below me—whales, fishes, and giant sea turtles floating effortlessly.

I see playful dolphins jumping around us.

Even the sea creatures acknowledge and worship Jesus.

There are beautiful colors in the sea, as the sun's rays dance along the water's surface.

After some time spent enjoying all the sea life's beauty, Jesus leads us back to the shore.

I tell Him that was the most awesome experience, and He says,

"Yes, I know when you were well and could come to the sea, how you loved it so.

In the quiet solitude of the waves, in your thoughts, you would always find Me,

Although I was never far from you."

Now, the day is becoming late afternoon in my wonderful dream.

Beautiful shades of orange, pink, purple, and gold melt across the sky,

as if a painter is brushing colors across the fading light.

It is the most magnificent sunset I have ever seen.

We have a picnic supper on the beach—Jesus, Pele, and me.

The food tastes so good; it is as if it were sent from heaven.

As I look into the eyes of Jesus, I tell Him that I am so thankful for this time,

this perfect day with Him and with Pele, if only in my dream.

To be healed and feel no pain is such a gift.

I ask Jesus if we could take another walk and play in the water again before it is time to go.

"Of course, my beloved," He says.

As the sun begins to set, the colors in the sky become more intense and beautiful.

We walk along and step into the cool water of the sea.

We venture out farther and begin splashing, playing, laughing.

Pele is beside me, frolicking in the waves.

I have never been so happy, felt so free or safe, as I did with Jesus on that perfect day in my dream.

Suddenly, I trip and begin to fall into the deeper water, but Jesus catches me and says,

"The Lord your God goes with you; I will never leave you nor forsake you" (Deuteronomy 31:6).

Back upon the shore, I thank Jesus for this glimpse into a beautiful life with Him.

I tell Him I don't want to leave this pristine place and that I want to stay with Him.

Jesus responds, "It is not your time yet."

He also tells me to never be afraid of dying, "For it is in death that we truly start to live."

When we die, we leave our imperfect bodies and we go to a most beautiful place where

there is no suffering of any kind.

There is only beauty, love, and peace that our human minds could never imagine.

All sickness, all fears, and all tears will be no more.

I am becoming very tired, and I lay down on the warm sand with Pele snuggled beside me.

I remember Jesus leaning over and kissing me on the forehead, saying, "I love you, My precious child."

Once again, I fall into a deep sleep.

An angel carries me home from this perfect place where I met Jesus.

As I awaken, my body is wracked once again with severe pain.

I can hardly believe the dream I had—or was it a dream?

I quietly ask the angel if what I experienced was real or not real. The angel replied:

"Yes, it was all true. It is what is yet to come.

God gave you this beautiful dream to reveal to you that a beautiful life with Christ is waiting for you and for all after this life.

Do not be afraid for He, the Lamb of God, is always with you and has already overcome this world.

Your body will one day die, but you will have everlasting life in Christ and live with Him in paradise."

Eye has not seen nor ear heard nor have entered into the heart of man the things which God has prepared for those who love Him.
—1 Corinthians 2:9

For the Lamb who is in the midst of the throne will shepherd them and lead them to living fountains of waters. And God will wipe away every tear from their eyes.
—Revelation 7:17

Crystal Tears of Mourning

A Prayer of Suffering, Grief, Gratitude, and Friendship

God blessed me with your friendship when we met years ago. As our relationship grew, I came to love you so.

You suffered with immense health issues, as I do now. You were funny and loving and made me laugh.

Your warm hugs and big, bright smiles would brighten anyone's day. Now that you're gone, the world seems so dark and silent; there are no more words left to say.

Admiring your strength through all that you suffered, you constantly chose to see the good in life. You were a wonderful, kind, and caring friend, mother, and an amazing beloved wife.

Always thinking of others, no matter your life circumstance. I remember once I sent you a card, and you called me from your hospital room, so sick, barely audible, trying so hard to just get the words out to say, "Thank you."

I know how much effort that was for you, but despite your own illness, you were always asking me what you could do for me. Remember what I used to say? "Please, Bon, just pray for me."

Your faith in the Lord Jesus was so strong, as I remembered in all of our conversations. We continually spoke of not understanding why, in this life, we must suffer so. Recently, your life became too much and your suffering so great; therefore, I understood why you had to go.

I remember you always said you considered yourself blessed and you knew God had a plan, even if, in this life, we could never fully comprehend or ever begin to understand.

I remember our conversations about being kind to others and striving to be peacemakers in the midst of life's terrible storms. We spoke about the importance of forgiving others because life was short and of not holding onto bitterness and anger but releasing it—letting it go, trusting, and giving it to God our Father from whom all blessings flow.

You placed value on your relationships with your family and friends, as you and I both agreed no amount of wealth could buy happiness or restore back anyone's failing health.

One of God's many gifts He gave you, in addition to your kindness and compassion for others, was your talent for crafting and cooking. You loved baking and giving handmade gifts of love. Some were so delicious, and others were so beautiful because you spent so much time perfecting every small detail. To us, your friends and family, they were treasures because you made them and they were a part of you—true gifts—that came from your heart.

You loved collecting your snowmen, and I will miss seeing that warm, smiling grin on your face. Every Christmas, I always gave you one.

You were loved by so many; so many friends, you had. Now, when I look at your pictures, my heart is filled with happy, bittersweet memories that just make me sad.

I shed crystal tears of mourning for you, my friend, each one creating an ascending staircase into heaven, where I want to climb to see you just one more time to say "I love you" once again before you had to go. There, you would take my hand, and a glimpse of heaven to me you would show.

I never got a chance to say goodbye before the day you died. Upon finding out, I was devastated, and beautiful crystal tears of mourning for you I cried.

Your strength in the Lord never waned, as you did your best to always be grateful, continually thanking God for being blessed, all the while trying to just survive and not complain.

Can you see my crystal tears of mourning for you in heaven, Bon? You knew, through my own tears of suffering, heaven is a place I so desire to come.

I remember crying to you in such pain, expressing how I wanted to go there, to dwell within the beauty and peace of our Lord Jesus.

Now, you were chosen to go first—to be with our Lord, forever healed in His presence, basking in His unconditional love, beauty, and feeling His warm, radiant light. I can only imagine how wonderful you must feel now, enveloped in His holy, healing, peaceful presence and never-ending loving sight.

In our last conversation before you left for heaven, you shared with me how tired and weary you felt fighting against your sickness and your pain. You expressed to me how one person can only withstand so much and how you felt you'd had enough. Truly, your suffering and humility, my heart did it touch.

You spoke of being ready to go when the Lord called your name. When I heard that you had died, I wanted Him to call my name just the same.

You and I, we understood each other, because we both came from a place of extraordinary suffering, a bond we shared, each our own—now, I must continue to go on without you, my friend, alone.

My crystal tears of mourning are for you, Bon—a cleansing for my spirit yet representing such sorrow; my heart completely broken in two.

I know you are with Jesus now, and He has bestowed His unconditional love and healing grace upon you. My friends chose to leave me when I became disabled and ill with such agonizing pain, but you, Bon, were a constant, understanding, compassionate friend, willing to listen and always so kind.

You did not choose to leave me, your friends, or your family, as you didn't know that day you had to go—when God called you home. Yet, I wouldn't have tried to stop you, even if I had known.

You went home with Him, knowing your pain and suffering would be forever gone. I could never fault you for that, just wish I was there with you and my aunt, where we would all be smiling, happy again, and singing praises with the angels to Jesus our king.

Our Lord and Savior will help your dear loved ones move on, but you will never be forgotten. Grateful for the times we shared together; the beautiful memories, I will always treasure.

Crystal tears of mourning I will continue to shed, as your beautiful life on this earth is now done; always in my heart, I will be forever missing you, Bon.

*That is, that we may be mutually encouraged by
each other's faith, both yours and mine.*

—Romans 1:12

*Beloved, let us love one another, for love is from God, and
whoever loves has been born of God and knows God.*

—1 John 4:7

Jesus, Please Come to Me

A Prayer of Intense Suffering, Distress, Hope, and Faith in Our Lord Jesus Christ

Jesus, please come to me, for I am in my desperate hour of need.

Close to you, I wish to be, so you may set my mind and broken body free—

to travel with you to heaven and behold the unimaginable beauty and splendor for my eyes and weary soul to see.

This grueling pain and affliction so great is keeping me bound, as an isolated prisoner with an unrelenting hold on me, a constant struggle forever weighing me down.

Ravaging my body and mind, I am so weary and cannot possibly go on.

Please, Jesus, take my hand, reaching down from heaven to gently pick me up out of my severe anguish and suffering.

I feel all alone, frightened like a tiny bird standing on a branch. I see and want to walk to You, even crawl if I must, but the branch— is about to break.

Please, Jesus, save me, for I do not know how much more of this great affliction I can continue to take. The daily isolation, loneliness, and inability to control the pain that my body must endure is like a violent sea of continuous waves crashing over my head, knocking me down, time after time, as I struggle to stand. I reach out for You, Jesus, for Your strong and guiding, loving hand. In such a stormy sea, I will not survive if You do not hold on to and protect me.

Held captive in a damaged painful shell, please, Lord, have mercy and show me the way out of my suffering body, as my soul desperately wants to shed. I wish I could walk away from this terrible pain and the sorrowful tears to be with You, Jesus, instead.

Please come seek me out, Lord, and soften this burden I must bear. Many days, I truly want to die to escape this horrible disease and suffering, feeling alone and sad; I just don't care, for this cross I must carry is just too much for me to continue to uphold, realizing life can be cruel and ever so unfair.

I cry, and my soul—my very essence of being—longs to be with You, Jesus, in that wonderful, loving, and peaceful place. I dream of heaven often, of being escorted into Your glory by Your beautiful, comforting angels of peace, rescuing me in the stillness and darkness of the night. I want to now lay down my burdens and stop this earthly fight; I am ready to be ushered into glory—and behold You, Jesus, my Savior's radiant, warm, and peaceful light. There, I will witness comforting presence in You, my creator's loving sight.

Thank You, Jesus, for my material possessions of this world, for my little stuffed animals that I like to hold, and for comforting music to which I sit and listen to, as I write my thoughts and continued prayers to You, sometimes praying and writing all night.

Thank You, Lord, for these few brief moments of tranquility in a raging storm at sea that's waging a violent war and battling within the inside and outside of me. As I hold my soft animals in my hands, I once again thank You, Jesus, for my small borrowed pleasures in life. You, Lord, have always known my love and compassion for animals, of how they can calm me in times of overbearing strife, bringing a little smile to my face, while continuing on with the cruel obstacles of life.

I realize, gracious Lord, that You have allowed me these quaint, comforting, material treasures that I hold near and can visually see. However, truly I know they do not and cannot possibly compare to all the eternal riches of peace, beauty, comfort, and being with You in heaven's paradise of eternity.

You, Jesus, are my true comforter, and no earthly treasures can ever compare. As I struggle daily with chronic illness and pain, thank You for my special animals, most of whom are my only friends; many hours a day with me do they spend. I have come to realize all my possessions are on loan from You to me for however long my stay on this earth will be.

Everything we have belongs to You, and all things will one day return to You, just as heavenly angels will carry my soul to You when my journey of this life is complete. Our time on this earth is but a whispered song of the wind. We are only here for a little while, then gone once again. Just as a candle burns bright for a finite period, eventually, it dies, and the light will never again shine. Please, Jesus, I want my friends and my family to remember my life song when I've passed on.

This terrible suffering I have had to endure has made me realize my need and want for Your constant presence, Jesus, my Lord. I want to be an inspiration to others by sharing with them they are not alone in their suffering, just a person in a sea of millions in this world who suffer tragically with no cure. I am a faceless individual to many but someone who has true compassion for the sick and dying. I know and deeply understand the extreme darkness, disease, chronic pain, and prolonged suffering can cause. It wreaks havoc on the body and can warp even the most outgoing person's mind. If it weren't for you, Jesus, I would not be here at all.

My need for You is great, Lord. You are the only one who understands my chronic pain and hears my cries, out of the deepest depths
of my soul. My images of You, Jesus, are so warm, loving, and kind.
Please forgive the intense suffering and crying, as it can and often
does distort my fragile human mind.

My wish is that You would reach down from heaven with Your
strong, mighty hand and gently scoop me up into Your loving arms
and bring me to Your home, where no harm would ever come to me
and I would never cry or ever be in pain again. For You, Jesus, were
the sacrificial lamb who died for all my sins, and I will dwell in the
safety of Your eternal presence forevermore.

Please, Jesus, come to me and carry me through heaven's small
open door. Oh, how I cry and cry in agony, as nothing in this world
truly satisfies. When I can't get away from chronic illness and unrelenting pain, death seems to be so comforting, if it means spending
beautiful heavenly days with You. Jesus, my Lord, the perfect, selfless
lamb who was slain.

I have waited and longed for You my whole life. Please come
quickly and softly, taking my hand, for wherever You lead, I will
follow. Please hear my undying prayer and cry for You, O (my) Lord.
What do I do when life is just too physically painful to live anymore?
I look toward heaven, where there might be just one open door that I
could wearily crawl through to be with You, Jesus, my Lord.

Jesus, please come to me, for I am in my desperate hour of need.
Close to You, I wish to be, so You may set my mind and broken
body free—to travel with You to heaven and behold the unimaginable beauty and splendor for my eyes and weary soul to see.

This grueling pain and affliction so great is keeping me bound,
as an isolated prisoner with an unrelenting hold on me, a constant
struggle forever weighing me down.

Jesus, please come to me, bringing me home, where I'll live with You forever. No more pain, tears, or suffering will I ever have to endure or suffer any more doubt or fear. I will behold all Your glorious angels, and the beauty of heaven will be unparalleled to anything my mind could ever comprehend or ever hope to see. Jesus, I am here, please come to me.

You softly call my name, as I wearily turn to see You walking toward me—on the water of the angry, turbulent sea. I call out to You—Jesus, you are my only and greatest need; please come and save me!

Your warm embrace, soothing smile, and holy face set my mind and ever so painful body eternally free. Gently taking my hand with Your unconditional love, we walk together on the calming sea with You smiling and saying, "Do not be afraid, for I am here. Keep your eyes on Me, as I will escort you into heaven's most beautiful paradise, and there, you will spend eternity with Me."

> *Have mercy on me, Lord, for I am faint; heal*
> *me, Lord, for my bones are in agony.*
>
> —Psalm 6:2

> *And after you have suffered a little while, the God of all*
> *grace, who has called you to His eternal glory in Christ, will*
> *Himself restore, confirm, strengthen, and establish you.*
>
> —1 Peter 5:10

Lord, Please Hear My Cry

A Prayer of Intense Suffering, Adversity,
Hope, and Faith in Jesus Christ

I call out to You, Lord God, in my terrible need; please save me, hear my desperate plea.

I am in such agonizing physical pain and discomfort; I cannot possibly last one more hour.

Please, Lord, deliver me from my hell on earth and keep me safe from the pit; afraid of this continuing pain, my fear is truly great.

Feeling hopeless and so discouraged, I wonder which day for me could finally be it? I am but a poor sinner, acknowledging repentance for the broken promises and sin against You in thought, word, and deed. My mind and heart are ashamed; my body is human, and the flesh is so weak.

I want to bask in Your loving arms and the radiant light of You, Jesus, longing and yearning for Your saving grace. I forever want to receive Your acceptance and loving smile upon seeing Your holy face.

I am so tormented by pain. I feel I have no good left in me. I cannot eat or sleep due to the torturous physical pain, or even rest during the day. The physical pain twists my emotions, causing my own thoughts to turn against me, like the blowing wind that can never be caught, escaping quickly on a whisper through the strong trees, or like uncontrolled waves churning violently on a once peaceful, tranquil sea.

Obedience to You, Lord, I feel I've continued to fail, struggling with isolation, loneliness, pain, and the chronic disability my condition constantly entails. If only I had made different choices in my life, would I still be entrapped in the pain of the enemy's snare—enduring so much daily strife?

Just living each day—every moment is a constant daily struggle that I must continue to try to bear, realizing few people can even understand or really care.

Please make Your loving presence known to me, Jesus, for I fear I am so desperately lost. This pain and sickness is devouring my body and poisoning my soul, from which I can find no escape. The burning pain is so great that I just want to die.

Lord, have I just sealed my fate? I've pushed all away with complaining due to inescapable pain, fear, and tears that endlessly stream down my face, for people cannot fully grasp the magnitude of my suffering or ever possibly know.

Please, Lord, do not turn from me and my suffering soul, thus withholding Your unconditional love and unfailing grace. O Lord, please have mercy and deliver me out of my pain, suffering, misery, and fear. Please, Lord, quickly come and take my hand, calm my spirit, bring me peace, and forever to me draw near. Amen.

For I know the plans that I have for you, declares the Lord;
plans to prosper you and not to harm you,
plans to give you hope and a future.
Then you will call upon Me and come and
pray to Me, and I will listen to you.
You will seek Me and find Me when you seek Me with all of your heart.
I will be found by you, declares the Lord.

—Jeremiah 29:11–14

Lord, I Turn to You

A Prayer of Crying Out to Our Lord in the Midst of Great Physical Suffering

What do I do when physical pain becomes so overbearing that no one can ever understand what I'm going through?

Lord, I turn to You.

What do I do when there is no cure for the suffering I must endure and thoughts of escape, of sweet eternal slumber abound in my mind?

Lord, I turn to You.

What do I do when I'm only able to live moment by moment, sometimes only second by second, because the pain is so intense I constantly feel sick?

Lord, I turn to You.

What do I do when tears of despair fall from my face, like blankets of rain falling on a cool summer's eve, each drop representing a tear of pain?

Lord, I turn to You.

What do I do when everyone leaves me because of my illness and I'm left in isolation to battle the pain and loneliness, when all I can do is just fight to live another day?

Lord, I turn to You.

What do I do when I lose my identity to my illness and continue to suffer so much loss, while trying, at the same time, to be grateful for Your many blessings at any cost?

Lord, I turn to You.

What do I do when I desire so much to participate in life the way I used to but can't anymore because of such a severe, painful disability?

Lord, I turn to You.

What do I do when I watch everyone else live their life, when they cannot possibly relate to me just trying to stay alive?

Lord, I turn to You.

What can I do when it hurts to breathe, my body writhing in pain, and all I can do is cry, wanting it to end and go away?

Lord, I turn to You.

What do I do when I want to go to heaven to be forever wrapped up in Your loving arms, rather than to continue living each and every painful day, for in this world, I truly do not want to stay?

Lord, I turn to You.

What do I do when I want to leave my body because of agonizing pain and fly my spirit home to You in heaven?

Lord, I turn to You.

My heart and soul turn to You, Lord, to reach out and take my hand.

My body aches to see Your holy face—just to see You smile at me and to softly say, "Everything will be okay."

I pray for peace in my spirit that You, O Lord, would place Your healing hand upon me to calm the raging storm of pain inside my body and to hear Your loving voice when it tells me to "be still."

I turn to You, Lord, for healing my broken body and hopeless spirit. Please wrap Your loving arms around me, opening my eyes to believe in You with childlike faith. You are my eternal Father in heaven, and I am your little girl who cries out in insurmountable pain, asking for strength and endurance if, in this world, I am to remain.

I long to be with You, Father, in Your heavenly kingdom, which my eyes cannot on this earth see but with the truth that my heart and soul truly believes. Please teach me to be quiet and to listen for the answers to my unanswered prayers. I turn to You and ask for strength and that You draw near me with Your presence when I'm too weary to go on.

I want only to be with You in heaven, where I'll always be safe and will forever praise You with unending song. It's difficult when your body is failing with illness and pain, no one can help you, and you finally realize things in life will never be the same. Lord, I turn to You, trying to hold on day by day, but the light of hope grows dim as I start to fade away.

I turn to You, Lord, my rescuer. My mind torments me, for I do not like or recognize the negatively painful thoughts as my own. I thought I could endure the extreme disability and pain but am certain I cannot continue, just as sure as You send down the warm summer rain.

I want to come home to You and cry every night for You to hear my prayers. When morning comes, I do not want to wake here on earth but wish to open my eyes in heaven, where I'll see Your holy face, as You will grant me restoration and a new healing faith.

I am at a loss on how to cope—feeling as if I'm slowly dying a slow death, like a noose being tied around my throat. With severe pain and no sleep, no peace on earth can I seem to find. You alone, Jesus, are my only hope, for I fear I am on a dangerous, slippery slope.

If I should stumble and fall, I pray You will catch me and judge me not, whatever way eternal slumber may greet me, come what may.

Lord, I turn to You as I lay down at night and continue to pray. You, Jesus, know how on this earth I wish to stay, but the pain is becoming too much. No one can possibly imagine the torturous pain I must endure, for it cannot be seen upon my face. If I can't hold on, I pray, please, Jesus, hold onto me, never to become lost but to spend eternity in heaven with Thee. Amen.

And I am convinced that nothing can ever separate us from God's love.
Neither death nor life, neither angels nor demons,
neither our fears for today nor our worries about tomorrow—
not even the powers of hell can separate us from God's love.
—Romans 8:38–39

Unanswered Prayers

A Prayer of Deep Suffering, Sorrow, and Searching

Jesus, why have You not answered my prayers?
Are You even really there?
I cry to You in my painful sorrow, for I cannot shake this anger
in the midst of my suffering.
I just want to die—to be away from this world and be with You.
I do not want to be here anymore, suffer anymore, pretend any-
more, cry anymore.

Why are we put upon this earth?
Is it a test to see how much pain and suffering we can withstand?
Who am I, and why have You not answered my prayers?
The longing I have to come home to You, Jesus, I can hardly
put into words.

My body and mind are so tired of just surviving, not living,
just trying to make it through to the next day.
People's lack of empathy, their judgment and ignorance cause
me further isolation,
and that causes anger to well up deep within me.

I have tried to cover my pain and despair with things of this world,
but it doesn't make life any easier and doesn't even matter,
for You, Jesus, are eternal and this world is not.

Why is my faith being tested in this way?

When I think back on all the suffering I have endured, I am lost for words.

No one should have to suffer like this, but many people do.

Why, Lord, do You allow friends and family to leave me when I need them the most?

People say that they don't forget you, but they do.

We can journey through this life with others, but in the end, we each must walk our own road, however painful or sad it is.

What can I say to someone who judges my sickness by what they cannot see

or even begin to understand until they have lived it themselves?

I believe in You, Jesus, but I am truly at a loss when I think of the suffering

that I and many others are going through.

I pray to You, Lord, and try not to become bitter when You remain silent.

I feel as if I am failing some test that has been given to me.

I am increasingly discouraged, but there is still a small light of hope and faith deep inside me.

When I pray to You, Lord, I pray that You hear my prayer.

It is a personal request for my healing from this vile disease that leaves me suffering with so many painful and frightening symptoms that thoughts of death seem like a welcome relief from this endless torture of life.

My body cannot keep up anymore, for I need many medications through the day just to maintain some functionality. Unfortunately, the drugs have some unpleasant side effects.

I feel like a soldier going to battle, fighting a war every day.

I know that pain, tears, weakness, loss of mobility, breathing problems, anxiety, depression, and so much more are my enemies.

Why are my prayers not being answered?

When there is a war, there are always two sides.

People are angry at the other side and want to eradicate the opponent.

My day is like this: I am angry that I have no control over what my body does,

and that entraps my mind as I realize that none of what I suffer from is normal.

I hope that one day soon, my body will give out, and Your angels will come and take me home.

I used to pray for total healing, for the pain in my body causes constant stress.

Now I pray for You to take me home, for I don't wish for any more suffering.

I would not allow my companion animal to suffer like this;

why should it be any different for a human being?

I know that every day I wake up is, by Your grace, a gift.

Please, dear Lord, answer my prayers and take me to be with You.

I am tired of the pain, the tests, the hospital, the doctors, and the meds.

I feel trapped in this isolating prison of pain,

and I struggle through as best as I can and try to hold on to You.

My only source of happiness is the hope that I will be with You in heaven one day.

"For my thoughts are not Your thoughts, neither are
Your ways my ways" declares the Lord.
"As the heavens are higher than the earth, so
are My ways higher that your ways
and My thoughts higher than your thoughts."
—Isaiah 55:8–9 NIV

The Veil

A Prayer of Desperate Suffering, Loneliness, and Hope in Our Lord and Savior, Jesus Christ

Loneliness and pain swirl around me, always present, never absent—not even for a moment.

A black veil descends upon my body, never to escape its tormenting presence.

It slowly drains every bit of joy and life from me, once in a happier state.

I long for You, Jesus—reaching out to You in this darkness.

I look for the light, just one spark of hope so desperately I try to find.

I cannot see or feel Your presence near, yet Your Word proclaims promises of love and healing so clear.

Am I just blinded by the loneliness and endless sea of pain?

Is my faith not strong enough to see that You really are here with me?

So much pain, so many tears, so much terrible suffering that others cannot see.

Please, Jesus, hear my cry for help, my desperate, tearful pleas.

I'm so afraid of what the future will mean for me.

Please, Jesus, I humbly ask that You be near and hold my hand, for soon enough, my body will return to dust and sand.

My heart so fragile and ready to break; one more crack, and surely, it will disintegrate.

There's no escape from the darkness of the veil.

The pain is all-encompassing; it holds me from within.

Only You, Jesus, can lift this black veil from me.

The unrelenting pain sends me back to the bottomless well of tears I've come to know so well.

My world, once abundant and overflowing, now is small and limited,

with very few things left that I can do.

People, busy in their lives, have lots to do;

in isolation and loneliness, they forget about me, even though it's only a few.

Jesus, here's my heart, and here's my hand.

I offer them freely to You.

One day, I will lose myself in Your radiant love that will be as pure as a radiant white-winged dove.

Jesus, it is You who understands my every thought, my broken heart and unsurmountable pain

That, to others, I just can't begin to even explain.

In my prayers at night, can You hear Your child's desperate pleas?

Can you see the constant tears falling, falling, falling in silence while the rest of the earth sleeps?

I pray Thee, Lord Jesus, my soul to keep.

Oh, how I long to be ever so close to You in all my brokenness.

No one understands that I cannot move beyond this black veil of suffering that holds me continually hostage.

In my severe pain, I think of heaven and of being with You.

Of sin and death, You, Lord, tore the veil, breaking all the chains.

Thank You, Jesus, for giving me Yourself, the lamb, a snow-white veil of healing, free from all sorrow and pain.

Then Jesus said,
"Come to me, all of you who are weary and carry
heavy burdens, and I will give you rest.
Take My yoke upon you. Let Me teach you, because
I am humble and gentle at heart,
and you will find rest for your souls."

—Matthew 11:28–29 NLT

My Longing Heart

A Prayer of Suffering, Comfort, Praise, and Honor for Jesus

O God, You are my God, with deepest longing I will seek You.
—Psalm 63:1

Jesus, I need You; please draw near to me,
for the storms of life, in the form of continuous physical suffering,
knock me down daily, like waves pummeling a sailing ship.
Please take me as I am and meet me in this painful place,
where I live in isolation, loneliness, and fear.
Throughout my illness, I continue to wonder what Your will for my life is
and how I am to serve You, Lord, when the pain is so overbearing that I find it
difficult to even breathe.

It is for You, Jesus, and my longing for heaven that my heart continually aches.
I have beautiful thoughts of You and I, of Your comforting unconditional love.
I allow my mind to drift away to where I'm walking with You, Jesus, on a beautiful beach, where we are watching sunsets over the water.

Walking through the most beautiful fields of colorful fragrant flowers,
You command the sun to come out and further brighten our day.

I have thoughts of You taking me up to the highest mountaintop,
where we see the most breathtaking snowcapped mountains,
and at night, we gaze up and see the brilliant white twinkling stars dotting the darkness.
You show me cascading waterfalls and we feel the cool spray mist on our faces.
When I am with You, Jesus, I feel completely loved and safe
for You are my Lord and Savior, and my heart longs for You.

Dear Jesus, my life is a battle zone,
using all my energy to cope with the pain that is so draining.
I try to control my emotions, which range from anger to tears
to complete devastation of my life, which my illness is causing,
and the losses I must come to accept.

I realize my only hope is in You.
My heart aches and longs for You.
Please teach me to trust You, as I must navigate this difficult path.
My faith needs strengthening, as it is beaten down and small, like a mustard seed.
Please water and tend to it, as my shepherd,
so it would take root and grow into something beautiful and pleasing to You
despite my struggles.

You, Jesus, are my peace and hope in the midst of these storms,
my protector when I'm scared, and my friend, Abba Father, forevermore.

I lay down and stretch my arms and hands upward toward
heaven.
I cry out unto You, wanting You so desperately to reach down
and clasp my hands in Yours, pulling me up from the depths of
this pain
and out of this world of suffering.

I imagine myself as a child, running to You, Jesus;
You scoop me up in Your strong arms, hugging and smiling at
me.
I feel so loved in Your arms, and I know I will be forever safe.
I also see myself as a child sitting on Your lap, my head against
Your chest,
never wanting to leave You or ever be away from You.

I feel as though I have searched and my heart has longed for You
my whole life.
I surrender all that I am to You, Jesus, and pray that You are
always with me,
by my side, holding my hand.
No matter how much or how little I may have to offer You or
the world in my weakened state, my thoughts of You and of heaven
get stronger with each passing day.

I know You do not judge us by the world's standards;
Your love is unconditional for all of humanity,
for every single one of us here on earth.
You are hope for the hopeless, strength for the weary,
love for the unloved and forgotten, peace for the tormented,
goodness over evil, and a light in the midst of all darkness.
"You are the light of the world" (Matthew 5:14).

My heart longs for You, but the pain and illness have broken it
in two.

Please show mercy and guidance throughout my life,
until heaven, where I will then be joyfully with You.
It is only in Your presence, Jesus, that I may find true joy, peace,
healing, and rest.
You are my Savior, my friend, my Abba Father.
Despite my illness and limitations,
I will praise and worship You for who You are to me
and what You have done for me, my precious Lord. Amen.

Because Your loving kindness is better than life, my lips shall praise You.
So I will bless You as long as I live, I will
lift up my hands in Your name.
—Psalm 63:3–4

About the Author

Patti Davis, born in 1966, was a beautiful, vibrant, talented, and creative wife, daughter, and friend, who grew up in Frederick, Maryland. Her smile would light up a room!

As a child, Patti loved singing and playing the guitar, handbells, and the piano. She also loved writing, gymnastics, and animals. Her flair for writing was rewarded early with an award from *Ranger Rick* magazine for an article she submitted at just ten years old. She also received awards for her artwork, music, and gymnastics. While dyslexia made learning difficult and allergies made interacting with animals challenging, her life was exemplified by the words of one of her early favorite songs "The Impossible Dream." She didn't allow her difficulties to hold her back. Her hard work and perseverance led to her success in all areas she pursued. Her struggles led to great empathy for others who struggled.

A graduate of Governor Thomas Johnson High School and a cum laude graduate of Towson University, Patti loved music and bringing joy to others. She sang professionally with local groups and as a soloist. She was also an accomplished pianist. She served Frederick County Public Schools, as a caring, dedicated elementary music educator for many years. She took great pride in helping her students learn and prepare for amazing performances.

Patti married Douglas Davis on April 26, 2003. When not singing, Patti loved to travel with her husband, Doug. Hawaii, Walt

Disney World, and Williamsburg were some of her favorite places. She loved swimming, snorkeling, going to concerts, and celebrating Christmas and other holidays with her family and friends.

Debilitating effects of what was initially diagnosed as fibromyalgia and later as Ehlers-Danlos syndrome (EDS) stole many of Patti's passions over the last twenty years of her life—her ability to sing, teach, travel, walk, and even just independently live each day. EDS is a very painful, degenerative, genetic disorder, which impacts connective tissue, joints, skin, and blood vessels.

The daily pain that Patti faced was often all-consuming and more than she could bear. Her faith in God, the unwavering support of her husband, Doug, and her family, and the unconditional love of her companion white schnauzers were what sustained her during these incredibly difficult years.

In Patti's loneliness and pain, she would call out to God—often late at night, when all others were asleep. Although not able to use her beautiful voice to sing, God blessed her with the ability to record her thoughts, feelings, and prayers in a way that has served to inspire and comfort others who suffer or who care for those who suffer. While not understanding her plight and constantly praying for healing, she was grateful that God used these struggles to draw her closer to Him.

Although her life ended much too early in 2020, at age fifty-four, due to complications from COVID-19, her hope and the hope of her family was that her prayers and writings would live on to comfort and support others who suffer and point them to the love of her precious Lord and Savior, Jesus Christ.